Last Minute Revision in PHARMACOLOGY

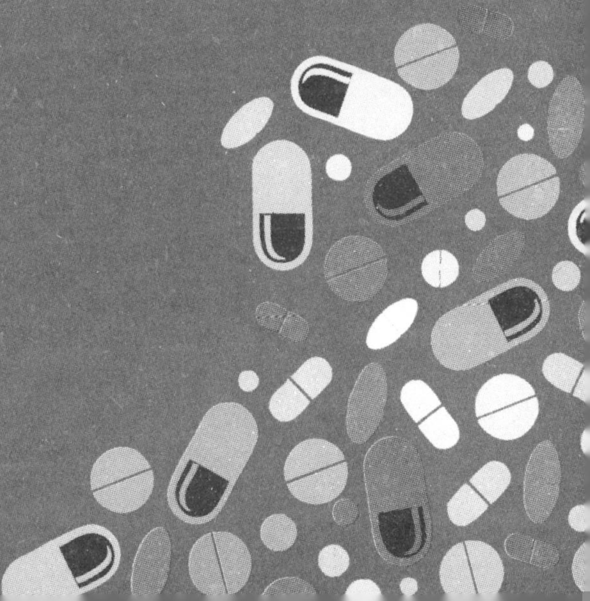

As per NEET/DNB/AIIMS/PGI Pattern

Last Minute Revision in PHARMACOLOGY

Dr. Vikas Dhikav (MBBS, MD, PhD)

Post Graduate Institute of Medical Education and Research (PGIMER), GGS-IP University, New Delhi, India
Ex-Resident & Senior Research Officer
Deptt. of Pharmacology
All India Institute of Medical Sciences, New Delhi, India
Visiting Honorary Professor,
ISM-IUK Kyryzstan (Erstwhile USSR) and Lugansk, Ukraine
Visiting Faculty, SMU, Nanchang, Dali, Luzhou, Ningbo, People's Republic of China

AITBS Publishers, India

MEDICAL PUBLISHERS

J-5/6, Krishan Nagar, Delhi-110051, INDIA
Phone: 011-40167052, 49067602
E-mail: aitbsindia@gmail.com & aitbsindia@hotmail.com

First Edition : 2006
Second Edition : 2009
Third Edition : 2013
Fourth Edition : 2027

ISBN: 978-81-7473-355-9

Published by:
Virender Kumar Arya for
AITBS Publishers, India
Medical Publishers
J-5/6, Krishan Nagar, Delhi-110051, INDIA
Phone: 011-40167052, 49067602
E-mail: aitbsindia@gmail.com & aitbsindia@hotmail.com

Printed by AITBS, Delhi

Preface to 4th Ed.

Last Minute Revision in PHARMACOLOGY is a popular book for over a decade now. The new edition contains updated version new key points for better understanding. Whole hearted thanks for accepting this small book as a part of MBBS/Pre-PG curriculum! This time, your favouraite book has grown up in size. As its earlier editions, it is useful as a rescue book for examination preparations. It is especially useful for VIVA and for revision during clinical rounds too. For preparing theory examination also, it is a good tool.

This edition contains more MCQs, especially NEET pattern. It also contains a small sections of MUST know points just before examinations. Three new chapters on contraception, clinical trials and emergency drugs have been included for better understanding. Please feel free to write to me for feedback or questions.

Vikas Dhikav

Preface to 2nd Ed.

'Last Minute Revision in Pharmacology' is meant be a simple, concise yet comprehensive book for quick revision of the subject. It will be useful not only for the beginners but also for the advanced students. First edition received over whelming support. I thank readers for their interest in the book. I thank Dr. Arjun Singhal for his help in editing the book.

Vikas Dhikav

LIST OF ABBREVIATIONS USED IN THE TEXT

DOC ------- Drug(s) of choice

TOC -------- Treatment of choice

GIT --------- Gastro-intestinal tract

BP ---------- Blood pressure

MAO ------ Mono amine oxidase

BZDs ------ Benzodiazepines

EPS -------- Extrapyramidal symptoms

ET ---------- Endotracheal intubation

CHF -------- Congestive heart failure

HTN ------- Hypertension

ACE -------- Angiotensin convertase enzyme

CCBs ------- Calcium channel blockers

IHD -------- Ischemic heart disease

PSVT ------ Paroxysmal supraventricular tachycardia

TCADs ----- Tricyclic antidepressants

SSRIs ------ Selective serotonin reuptake inhibitors

SNRI ------- Selective norepinephrine reuptake inhibitors

NMDA ---- N-methyl D-asparate

GTCS ------ Generalized tonic clonic seizures

ACTH ------ Adrenocorticotropic hormone

SE --------- Side effect(s)

PD --------- Parkinson's disease

TMP-SX2 - Trimethoprim-puephametuoxazole
COMT ----- Catechol-o-methyl-transferase
OCD ------- Obsessive compulsive disorders
NSAIDS --- Non-steroidal anti-inflammatory drugs
PPIs ------- Proton pump inhibitors (H^+K^+ pump inhibitors)
COX-2 ----- Cyclo-oxygenase
ENT -------- Ear\nose\throat
LA --------- Local anaesthetic
GA --------- General anesthetic
MC --------- Most common/most commonly
ECT -------- Electroconvulsive therapy
AMI ------- Acute myocardial infarction
Tb --------- Tuberculosis
GH --------- Growth hormone
GERD ------ Gastroesophageal reflux
RAI -------- Radioimmunoassay
FQ --------- Fluoroquinolone
MDR ------ Multi-drug resistant
ALL -------- Acute lymphocytic leukemia
CLL -------- Chronic lymphocytic leukemia
AML ------- Acute myelocytic leukemia
CML ------- Chronic myeloid leukemia

Contents

Unit 1

General Pharmacology

Availability of newer drugs doesn't mean that old were bad—Confucious

MEDICAL PHARMACOLOGY

General Pharmacology

- **Pharmacology (pharmakon-drug; logos-study)** has two arms; pharmacokinetics and pharmacodynamics. The former means movement of the drugs while the latter means mechanism of drug action.
- **Pharmacokinetics** has four main parts; absorption, distribution, metabolism and excretion (ADME). It means how does the body handle the drug.
- Most common mode of drug absorption is **passive diffusion (not saturable);** Methyldopa and levodopa are two drugs undergoing active absorption (hence saturable). Absorption of levodopa is reduced by protein meal.
- **Lipid solubility** is the most important determinant of drug absorption. Water-soluble drugs are absorbed from the pores present in between the cells. More the lipid solubility; more is the rate and extent of the drug absorbed.
- Drugs are given by two main routes: oral and parenteral.
- **Oral route** is the oldest route of drug delivery; many drugs like aminoglycosides are not ab-

sorbed. Others like penicillin G and methicillin are acid labile. **Acid labile** drugs get destroyed by pH of stomach hence can not be given by oral route. Food normally interferes with absorption of most drugs but many are more absorbed in presence of meals and these include; *griseofulvin, halofantrine, carbamazepine, hydrochlorothiazide, nitrofurantoin* and *lithium*.

- Some drugs like *hydrochlorothiazide, doxycycline, halofantrine, minocycline, clindamycin, fluoroquinolones* have 100% bioavailability despite the presence of food.
- Drugs like nicotine, nitroglycerine and nifedipine are given sublingually to avoid hepatic *first pass* metabolism.
- **Prochlorperazine** and **midazolam** are drugs given by buccal route. It is less reliable as the area between gums and lower lips is not highly vascular.
- Drugs of high molecular weight, especially proteins are given by IV route; bioavailability is 100% by this route. Intramuscular route is used for drugs with formulated in oily vehicles. Irritant drugs can be given. Bioavailability by SC route is intermediate between intravenous and intramuscular route.

- Drugs given via intra-arterial route escape first pass metabolism in lungs. This route is used for cancer treatment and angiographies.
- Transdermal patch is a specialized form of drug delivery used to ensure smooth plasma concentrations while avoiding the drug to be taken regularly. Nitrate patches for angina and fentanyl patches for postoperative pain are popular.
- **Bioavailability** means the amount of drug reaching into blood in an unchanged manner. It depends upon **tablet size, force** in preparation of tablets and **first pass** metabolism. It is calculated mathematically by estimating the area under curve.

$$\text{Levodopa} \xrightarrow[\text{Dopa decarboxylase}]{B_6^+} \text{Dopamine}$$

Figure: ***Metabolism of levodopa in wall of gut. Since, B6 is a cofactor for the enzyme dopa decarboxylase; therefore, it is not given along with L-dopa.***

- **First-pass metabolism** means drug metabolism before a drug reaches to the circulation. It occurs in wall of gut and liver. Importantly, wall of the gut is rich in metabolic enzymes. Some drugs like chlorpromazine are metabolized here.
- In some instances, it depends upon rate of blood flow. Examples include, **lidocaine, propranolol and nitroglycerine (PNL=acronym; profit N**

loss). More the blood flow would mean more metabolism and hence less bioavailability. In case of CHF, however, the bioavailability would be more due to less blood flow and less metabolism. Consequently, dose of drugs like lidocaine needs reduction in CHF.

- Similarly, when propranolol is used with lidocaine; dose of lidocaine should be **reduced** as propranolol reduces the hepatic blood flow (by almost 40%) thereby creating a CHF like situation.
- **Distribution** means spread of drug, while *redistribution* means that a drug goes to a highly perfused organ first followed by plasma. It is seen in case of drugs like *thiopentone* and *midazolam*. **Redistribution** is a mechanism of termination of pharmacological activity **(metabolism). Drugs undergoing redistributing are short acting.**
- **Volume of distribution (Vd)** is hypothetical volume in which the drug appears to be distributed. Half-life is directly proportional to volume of distribution and inversely related to clearance. Vd helps us in estimating the half-life of the drug, rough duration of action and location of the drug (if Vd is low the drug is in plasma; if Vd is high, it is outside plasma). Importantly, drugs with large volume of distribution have long duration and vice versa.

- Some drugs are distributed to particular organs like eye. For example, **amiodarone** causes corneal micro-deposits; **ethambutol** interferes with **red** and **green vision, digoxin** with **yellow vision**, and **Thioridazine** with **brown vision.**

- **Clearance (Cl)** is the volume of plasma that gets filtered of the drug in unit time. Clearance is additive and when the term Cl is used it means bile and renal both. It is calculated by the formula:

$$Cl = \frac{\text{Rate of elemination}}{\text{Plasma cocentration}}$$

- It is of two types–**zero order** (amount constant) also known Michaelis Menton kinetics, or dose dependent elimination) and **first order** (fraction constant).

- Both **half-life** and **Cl** remain constant in first order kinetics while both change in zero order.

$$t_{1\backslash 2} = \frac{0.693 \times Vd}{Cl}$$

- Half-life is time taken by the drug to reduce its concentration by half. **A drug is eliminated completely in 4-5 half-lives. 90% of the drug is eliminated in 3-4 half-lives. Half-lite can tell us about the time to achieve** *plasma steady state concentration* (*PSSC*). **This can be calculated by multiplying the half-life of the drug to a fac-**

tor of 5 (time PSSc = t½ x 5). Half-life can not calculate the drug dose. Importantly, dosages of the drugs are calculated by the formulas given below:

- **Loading dose** is dose required to produce **Pssc** rapidly = (Vd x desired concentration); **maintenance dose** (Cl x desired concentration).
- Loading dose may be needed in emergency; **so if we want to achieve plasma steady state concentrations quickly;** we can use loading dose.

  Loading dose = Vd × Concentration

  Maintenance dose can alternatively be calculated by the formula:

  Clearance × Concentration

  Maintenance dose is modified in renal failure, not loading dose.

  Corrected dose is used in case of renal impairment. This is calculated by:

$$\frac{\text{Average dose} \times \text{Patient's creatinine clearance}}{\text{Normal creatinine clearance}}$$

- **Teratogens** are drugs that cause organ mal-formations; given below is the list of important teratogens.

Table: Some teratogens

- **Thalidomide:** Phocomelia
- **Valproic acid:** Spina bifida (neural tube defect)*
- **Estrogens:** Adenocarcinoma of vagina
- **Testosterone:** Masculinization
- **Phenytoin:** Microcephaly, cleft palate and lip
- **Isotretinoin:** Cleft palate, Cleft lip
- **Alcohol:** Microcephaly
- **Lithium:** Ebstein anomaly
- **Carbamazepine:** Scalp defect, hypothyroidism, choanal atresia and anaplasia cutis
- **Misoprostol:** Moebius syndrome

- Period between 17th to 54th days is most vulnerable as organogenesis occurs during this period. Teratogenicity is most likely.
- **Therapeutic index** is the ratio between effective dose **(LD50/ED50)** to lethal dose in 50% of animals. It is an indicator of drug **safety** and is the initial test during drug development.
- **Ames test** is used for carcinogenicity and involves the uses of *Salmonella Typhimurium*. This test measures the ability of the drug to produce mutation. Therapeutic drug monitoring is needed in case of such drugs.

---

*It can be prevented by folic acid administration

- **Therapeutic window** means that drug exhibits pharmacological response is a narrow dose range. Nortriptyline, digoxin, glipizide etc. are examples of drugs having this effect. Some authors use both terms equally.
- **Dose response curve** is the relationship between log of dose and response.

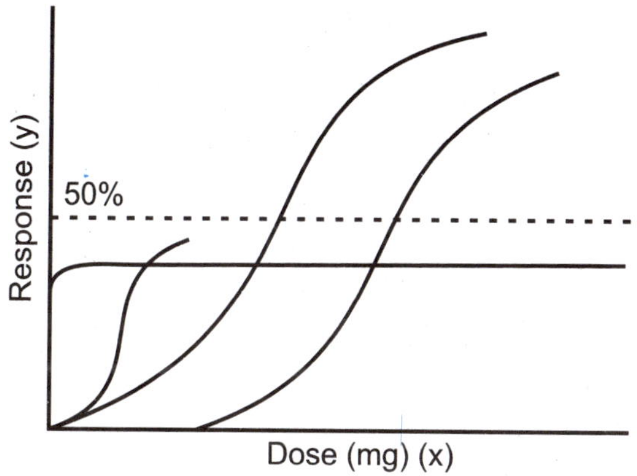

- Slope indicates **safety**, X-axis indicates **potency** and height of DRC indicates **efficacy**.
- Partial agonists produce **blunted** response of *DRC, parallel and rightward shift indicates* competitive antagonism and irreversible antagonists produce flattening of DRC.
- A **partial agonist** can become full agonist if the number of spare receptors are large or if it is used with an irreversible antagonist.

- **Spare receptors** are present in a number over and above the usual number and impart the physiological responsiveness to the tissues.
- Drug action can be prolonged by **increasing the dose, slowing excretion** (probenecid **reduce excretion** of penicillins), **reducing metabolism** (cilastin reduce metabolism of imipenem) and **producing vaso-constriction** (e.g. adrenaline and lidocaine). Using sustained release is a common mode of drug action.

  Importantly, using enteric-coated preparations is not a mode of prolongation of drug action. Use of vasoconstrictors can prolong the duration of drug action due to reduced absorption from site of action.

  Side effects are undesirable but unavoidable accompaniments of drug treatments. They are of five types (see below).

Table: Types of sid eeffects

- **Type-A:** Augmented (dose dependent; more side effects at high doses)
- **Type-B:** Bizarre (dose independent, genetically determined, idiosyncratic)
- **Type-C:** Chronic (continuous use causes them, e.g. tardive dyskinesia)

- **Type-D:** Delayed (May occur even long after discontinuation)
- **Type-E:** End of dose (e.g., end of dose dyskinesia)

- **Clinical trials** are human experiments designed to test the drug experimentally for clinical use. They test safety, efficacy and tolerability of drug.

Table: Phases of clinical trials

- **Phase-1:** Done in healthy volunteers (20-50; tests pharmacokinetics and safety)
- **Phase-2:** Done in healthy volunteers (100-300; confirms pharmacokinetics and safety-further evaluation)
- **Phase-3*:** Done in patients (300-1000; tests clinical efficacy, involves patients and null hypothesis may be rejected) efficacy is also evaluated.
- **Phase-4:** Also called post-marketing surveillance (done in out and in-patients, does not require ethical clearance). A new term for this is pharmacovigilance.

*NDA (New Drug Application) may be submitted for FDA approval.

Unit 2

Autonomic Nervous System

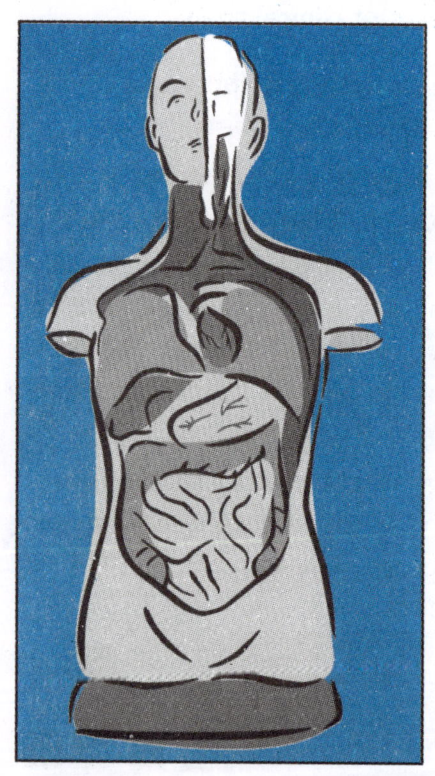

Learn to unlearn

—Benjamin Disreali

INTRODUCTION

- **Autonomic Nervous System** is concerned with autonomic activity; father of ANS pharmacology is **Langley**, a British Pharmacologist.
- ANS has three main divisions, sympathetic, parasympathetic and enteric nervous system.
- **Sympathetic cholinergic fibers** are present in sweat glands; **non-adrenergic non-cholinergic fibers** are found in male reproductive tract like prostate, epididymis and seminal vesicles. *Non-adrenergic* and *non-cholinergic fibers* are present in male reproductive tract e.g. prostate, seminal vesicle and epididymis.
- **Botulinum toxin** reduces release of acetylcholine; hemicholiniums are drugs *inhibiting* the synthesis of acetylcholine by inhibiting choline up take.
- Acetylcholine is metabolized by true (neuronal enzyme) and false pseudocholinesterase-present in liver, plasma, stellate cells (deficiency causes apnea if given succinylcholine). Deficiency can be diagnosed by **dibucaine number test.**

- **Bethanechol** (direct acting cholinomimetic) is used in Hirschsprung's disease, achalasia cardia and post-operative urinary retention. It is mainly a muscarinic agonist and is selective for bowel and bladder. Therefore, it is used for treatment of postoperative urinary and bowel obstruction.
- **Methacholine** has only muscarinic actions, while carbachol has mainly nicotinic actions. Latter is selective for bladder and gut.
- **Carbachol** has got direct and indirect (**mixed**) actions; therefore, it should **not** be given by intravenous route. It acts upon mostly, nicotinic receptors. The drug has lusitropic action (atrial relaxation).
- **Neostigmine** (quaternary amine) is DOC for reversal of non-depolarizing block, **cobra-bite** and **myasthenia gravis.** It is **ineffective** for depolarizing block (succinylcholine) and is **contraindicated** in case of block by mivacurium shortest acting non-depolarizing blocker ($t_{½}$ = 10-20 min). This is because, both of them are metabolized by *pseudocholinesterase*; an enzyme **inhibited** by neostigmine.
- Neostigmine has got both nicotinic and muscarinic actions. It stimulates the nicotinic and gan-

glionic receptors; therefore it can increase blood pressure. So sometimes, it can mimic the effects of ganglion stimulation. Neostigmine is the anticholinesterase **agent of choice** for treatment of paralytic ileus or urinary bladder atony.

- **Edrophonium** is a carbamate with alcoholic group. It is the shortest acting carbamate ($t_{½}$ = 10-20 minutes). It acts reversibly and is the DOC for differentiating between muscarinic from cholinergic muscle weakness.

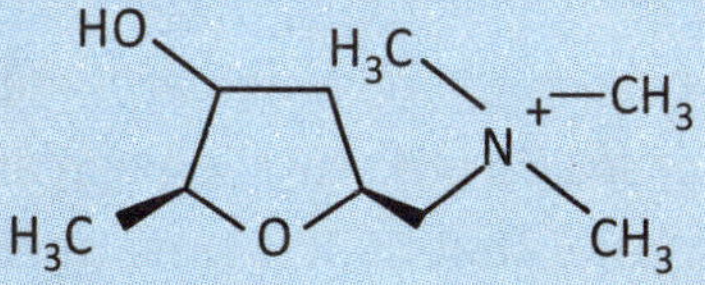

Figure: ***Muscarine: the model alkaloid***

- Physostigmine is DOC for **belladonna poisoning**, as it is tertiary amine and penetrates blood brain barrier freely. This is due to its lipid solubility. Its rare side effect is respiratory depression (cf neostigime).
- **Pilocarpine** is cholinomimetic alkaloid used for glaucoma. However it is no longer DOC (current DOC-timolol) for primary open angle glaucoma because is causes meiosis and cyclospasm and control of IOP. Presence of inflammatory eye dis-

ease and retinal detachment are **contra-indications** of anti-glaucoma medications.

- **Timolol** can cause blephroconjuctivitis while latanoprost ($PGF_{2\text{-alpha}}$) can cause iris pigmentation and growth of eyelash hairs.
- DOC for **organophosphate poisoning** is atropine; cholinesterase re-activators (called as oximes) e.g. pralidoxime, obidoxime are also used. *Pralidoxime* has peripheral action while obidoxime has central effects. Antidote of choice is pralidoxime.
- Oximes are **ineffective** in carbamate poisoning. These drugs do not work if given after 24 hours; the reason is that by this time *ageing* has developed. Therefore, it becomes difficult to separate the enzyme-organophosphate complex.
- **Donepazil** is the DOC for Alzhiemer's disease (AD), an organic brain disease (MC cause of dementia); occurs due to acetylcholine deficiency (Other drugs-tacrine, matrifonate, rivastigmine, galantamine etc.). Matrifonate was used in past as antischistosoma drug. Memantine is NMDA receptor blocker used in advanced AD.

ANTICHOLINERGIC DRUGS

- Atropine (belladonna alkaloid) is **muscarinic** receptor antagonist. It also antagonizes nicotinic receptors but at high dosages. At **normal therapeutic** doses, it does not cross blood placental and brain barrier.

- **Atropine** is contraindicated in *amanita muscaria* poisoning but is the DOC for *inocybe* poisoning. It has no role in delayed type of poisoning that is a neurodegenerative disease managed by thiocetic acid.

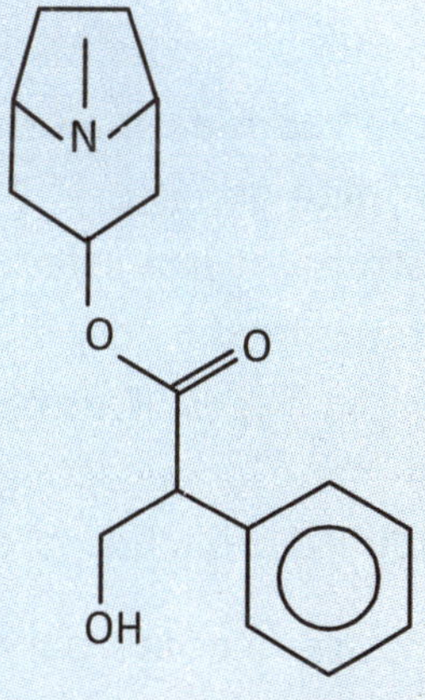

Figure: ***Atropine structure***

- Atropine is also the DOC for producing dryness of respiratory secretions, vagal bradycardia (**sinus bradycardia**), reducing salivary secretions (anti-sialogogue), carbamate poisoning and organophosphate poisoning). **Suxamethonium**, **halothane** and **neostigmine** are common causes of intra-operative bradycardias for which atropine can be used.

- Atropine is the **longest** acting mydriatic agent (duration 1 week) and is the agent of choice for children **(2% ointment).** Fever is the most common side effect of atropine in children. In adults, it is dryness of mouth. For routine fundal examination only mydriasis is sufficient, while for detailed examination both mydriasis and cycloplegia is needed.
- **Ipratropium bromide** is a semisynthetic derivative of atropine and is useful both in acute and chronic asthma. It is a selective M3 blocker its use is accompanied by dry mouth and is treated by nystatin lozenges. **Tiotrophium** is more selective, safer and longer acting. It is DOC for beta-blocker induced bronchospasm.
- **Glycopyrrolate**, a quaternary amine is atropine substitute especially useful for older patients undergoing surgery. It is more cardio-stable; it is selective M3 blocker and is devoid of central anticholinergic effects.

- **Pipenzolate** is used for infantile colic, while flevoxate is used for ureteric colic-drug of choice is **diclofenac sodium.** Morphine should be avoided in renal colic as it is an opioid and can provoke biliary spasm.

- **Hyosine butylbromide** (Buscopan) is used commonly as anticholinergic drug for abdominal pain of spasmodic type. Drotaverine is used commonly now a days; it is a phosphodiesterase inhibitor.

- **Dicyclomine** has both antiemetics and anti-motion sickness property. It is commonly used as anti-spasmodic drug.

- **Hyoscine** (levo-scopolamine) is DOC for motion sickness and has amnesic properties (was used Postworld War-II to produce amnesia) it is most lipid-soluble anticholinergic drug and causes initial bradycardia due to blockade of presynaptic M1 receptor.

- **Oxybutinin and tolterodine** (DOC) are anti-cholinergic drugs used in unstable bladder as they relax detrusor muscle and increase capacity of urinary bladder. Most common side effect of oxybutinin is **dry mouth.**

- **Trospium, derifenacin** and *solifenacin* can also be used. These are more selective and longer acting compared to rest of the drugs. Scopolamin has amnesia causing action and is used in the treatment of motion sickness. However, thiopentone is the drug of choice for lie detection (Narcoanalysis).

ADRENERGIC DRUGS

- **Noradrenaline** is the predominant catecholamine produced by sympathetic neurons, while adrenaline is produced by adrenal medulla. **Tyrosine-hydroxylase** is rate limiting step in catecholamines biosynthesis, while mono amine oxidase (MAO), COMT (Catacol-O-Methyl-Transferase) metabolize catecholamines to vanillyl-mendalic acid (VMA) as main metabolite.

- **Adrenaline** is DOC for angioedema, anaphylactic shock, and **cardiac arrest.** In cardiac arrest, it acts by increasing the frequency of impulse generation. Dose is 0.2-0.5 ml (dilution 1:1000) given subcutaneously, repeated 3 times if needed. Arrhythmia are most common serious side effects.

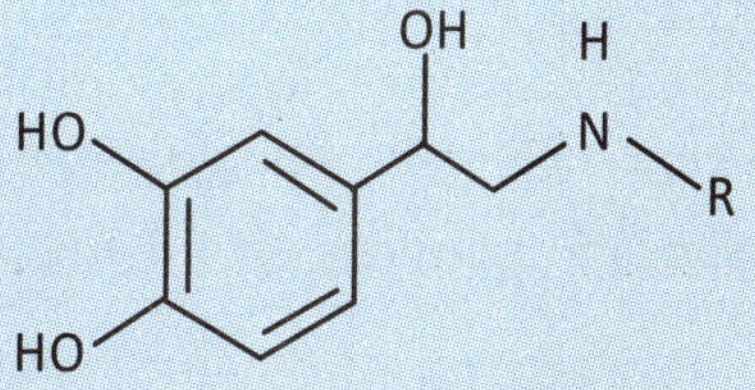

Figure: *Adrenaline*

- **Norepinephrine** (α_1, α_2, β_1 actions) **increases** blood pressure severely and causes narrow pulse pressure, as the drug is a powerful vasoconstrictor. Bradycardia occurs as a result of increase BP. But in transplanted heart, the heart rate increases because vagal fibers are removed during heart transplant. It is sometimes used as a **styptic** (drugs arresting local bleed). It does not act upon β_2 receptors.

- **Isoproterenol** (β_1 agonist-pure sympathomimetic) is DOC for heart block (Causes pure rise of systolic BP, while diastolic BP decreases. It is the fastest acting bronchodilator that is safe in pregnancy. It increases the SBP but diastolic BP decreases. This widens the pulse pressure and heart rate increases. It is the DOC for acquired *torsa de depointes* and heart block. It used to be a popular drug for bronchial asthma. But now a days, it is not used due to availability of better agents.
- **Mepheneteramine** (alpha agonist) is DOC for short-term rise of BP; while **ephedrine** is the DOC for fall of BP following spinal anesthesia.
- **Dopamine** acts on D1 receptors in kidney (renal vasodilator)-Haloperidol reduces the renal effects. Effects are dose dependent. For example, 2-5 microgram\kg\min\IV is the renal dose. It exhibits beta-adrenergic stimulant effect in high dose.

- **Dobutamine** (beta1 agonist-does not act on dopamine receptors) is drug of choice for cardiogenic shock and is also used in pump failure (e.g., following AMI, heart surgery). Its half-life is 2-10 minutes and it is an inotropic agent that increases force of contraction but heart rate remains unchanged. Therefore, it would not be useful in beta-blocker induced bradycardia.

- **Phenylephrine** is the drug that produces **mydriasis without cycloplegia.** It is used in cough and cold preparations as a nasal decongestant. **Phenylpropanolamine** and pseudoephedrine also act similarly.

- Adrenaline also produces mydriasis but no cycloplegia. *Dipivefrine* is the prodrug that gets converted into adrenaline.

- Midodrine is **DOC** for postural hypotension. Ephedrine is an alternative. Midodrine can cause **supine hypertension** due to modulation of baroreceptors. Therefore, the drug is not taken in lying down position.

- Methylphenidate is **DOC** for attention deficit hyperkinetic disorders (ADHD); atomoxetine is a new drug for this indication.

- Imipramine is DOC for **nocturnal enuresis** due to its anticholinergic property; dry mouth, urinary retention and tachycardia are its important side effects. The drug decrease the bladder pressure and hence is used in this condition.

- Desmopressin is the current drug of choice for this indication.

ALPHA-BLOCKERS

- **Alpha-blockers** are of two types (selective and non-selective); Prazocin, terazocin are selective alpha1 blockers that do not cause **reflex tachycardia** as they do not increase release of norepinephrine. This is because; these do not block the postganglionic alpha receptors. Their most common side effect is postural hypotension. They are DOC for BPH with hypertension.

- **First-dose hypotension** is most common side effect of alpha-blockers; they do not increase lipid levels like beta-blockers-rather improve lipid profile. **Alpha-2** agonists too produce slight improvement in lipid profile.

- Phenoxybenzamine is the **drug of choice** for pheochromocytoma; beta-blockers are not given in pheochromocytoma before using alpha-blockers. It is also used for Raynaud's disease. This is due to unopposed vasoconstriction.

- Phentolamine is reversible alpha-blocker preferred in patients with pheochromocytoma undergoing surgery. It can also be used for necrosis and gangrene induced by thiopentone.

BETA-BLOCKERS

- P3 **(propranolol, pindolol and penbutolol)** are lipid soluble beta-blockers. These are well absorbed and enter into blood brain barrier easily. **ANS** (atenolol, nandolol, and sotalol) are water-soluble beta-blockers. These are longer acting, excreted unchanged from kidney and are contraindicated in presence of renal failure. They do not enter the blood brain barrier; hence they are free from the usual CNS side effects of beta-blockers (e.g., insomnia and depression).
- **Nadolol** is the longest acting beta-blocker (t½ = 24 hours) while atenolol is the beta-blocker with **minimum protein binding.** Propranolol has highest hepatic first pass metabolism, high protein binding and is maximally metabolized beta-blocker. Propanolol is beta blocker with maximum lipid solubility and high protein binding.
- Esmolol is **shortest** acting beta-blocker ($t_{½}$ = <10 minutes); metabolized in plasma therefore is safe in renal/hepatic failure (atenolol is longest acting beta-blocker). Other drugs metabolized by plasma esterases are procaine, chloroprocaine and remafentanil.

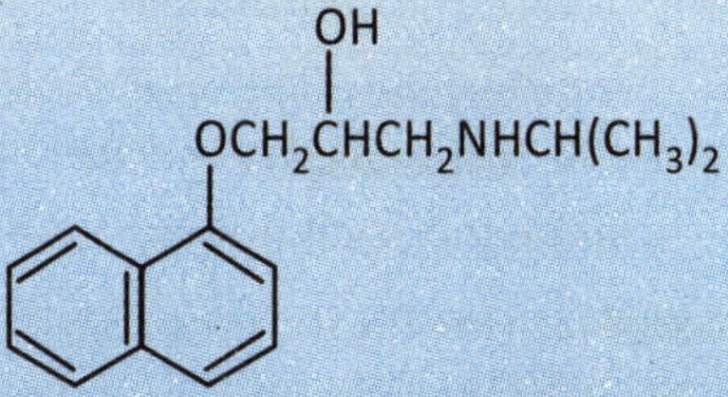

$$\text{OCH}_2\text{CH(OH)CH}_2\text{NHCH(CH}_3)_2$$

Figure: *Propranolol*

- **PALM** (Propranolol, Pindolol, Alprenolol, Labetalol, Metoprolol) are beta-blockers with local anesthetic activity (membrane stabilizing activity). Alprenolol has maximum membrane stabilising activity.
- MC side effect of beta-blockers is **bradycardia**; they can also cause AV nodal block, depression, suicidal tendencies, nightmares, hyperlipidemia, impotence and worsening of asthma, diabetes and peripheral vascular disease. Verapmil/ Diltiazem should not be combined with beta-blockers.
- All non-selective blockers (propranolol, sotalol, nandolol, and timolol) are contraindicated in pregnancy while cardioselective (atenolol, metoprolol, Bisoprolol, betaxalol and esmolol) are *safe* in pregnancy.
- Beta-blockers with **intrinsic sympathomimetic properties**-ISA (Alprenolol, oxprenolol, pindolol,

carteolol, celiprolol, penbutolol) have NO adverse effect on lipid profile and they do not cause bradycardia. **Labetalol** is the only drug outside this group having such activity.

- **Carvidilol** (antioxidant property), *labetalol* (DOC for aortic dissection) and *dilevalol* (isomeric drug) are combined acting beta-blockers. Combined blockers have vasodilator activity (otherwise, beta-blockers are NOT vasodilators).
- **Beta-blockers** reduce the blood pressure by *decreasing* cardiac output. This reduces the sympathetic activity which could reduce the vasoconstrictor outflow to the blood vessels. Nebivolol is beta-blocker with cardio selective nature (β_1). It is beta-blocker with vasodilator activity.

Unit 3

Cardiovascular Drugs

Hope is one of the best medicine

—A Proverb

ANTIANGINAL DRUGS

- Angina develops as a result of imbalance between oxygen supply and demand. Drugs that reduce oxygen demand or dilate coronaries (increase coronary blood flow) improve symptoms of angina. Double product (Systolic BP × Heart Rate) can determine myocardial work done. Beta-blockers and nitrates *reduce* double products.
- Nitrates are the DOCs of initial choice for all sorts of angina pain. They contain nitrites as impurities (responsible for methaemoglobinaemia).
- Nitrates act by delivering NO (nitric oxide) and are mainly venodilators (through cGMP). Therefore, they reduce preload. However, they dilate renal arteries also therefore, they increase oxygen supply also. These are useful antianginal agents as the drugs reduce preload.
- Nitrates are lipid-soluble drugs but have extensive hepatic first pass metabolism. Isosorbide mononitrate is the longest acting nitrate with best oral bioavailability. It is also most commonly used oral nitrate for the same reason.
- Nitroglycerine is most lipid soluble nitrate, therefore, can be given sublingually or as a transdermal patch.

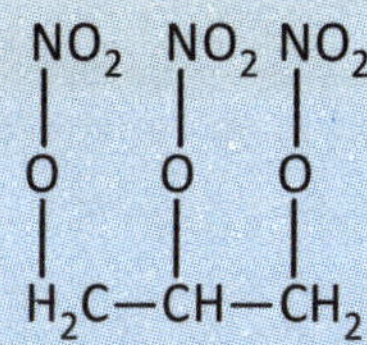

Figure: **Nitroglycerine**

- Beta-blockers act by reducing the force of contraction and hence decrease oxygen requirement. These are contraindicated in **variant angina** (would cause unopposed vasospasm).
- DOC for **variant angina** (also called Prinzmetal's angina/ST elevation angina) are CCBs-these are arterial dilatators. Verapmil is better than diltiazem for this indication.
- Most common side effect of nitrates is **pulsatile headache.** Postural hypotension occurs. Tolerance develops with nitrates on regular use. Intermittent use can prevent the tolerance development.
- Rare side effect of nitrates is **methaemoglobinaemia** and it is of therapeutic value. It occurs due to high amounts of **nitrites.** Amyl nitrite is the drug of choice for **cyanide poisoning.**

HYPERTENSION

- Hypertension is BP =140/90; emergency hypertension is defined as BP =210/120. **Veratrum alkaloids** act by increasing baro-receptor sensitivity and are obsolete. Similarly, ganglion blockers such as tripmethophan (past DOC for aortic dissection), hexamethonium and mecylamine are not used as they produce profound blockade of sympathetic and parasympathetic function.
- **Reserpine** is one of the oldest antihypertensive drug (Discovered by Indians named Sen and Bose in 1932) with neuron depleting and antipsychotic properties. It can cause mental depression upon chronic use that is why not popular.
- DOC for hypertension with BPH is terazocin/ prazocin.**Tamsulosin (selective alhpa-1A)** is the DOC for BPH. **Finasteride** is used mainly in patients with large prostates. It acts by inhibiting the conversion of testosterone to dehydro-testosterone (5-α reductase inhibitor).
- Alpha-blockers of selective type (Prazocin, terazocin) **do not** cause **reflex tachycardia** (non-selective type, e.g., phentolamine cause it). They are not used as sole antihypertensive agents.

Alpha-blockers and a agonists **do not deteriorate** blood lipid levels rather improve it (only antihypertensive improving lipid profile). Recall that beta-blockers **deteriorate** lipid profile.

- DOC for hypertension with angina is **beta-blocker** (Beta-blockers are DOC for HTN in stressed patients and those with high rennin levels).
- Direct acting **arterial dilators** include; diazoxide, hydralazine and minoxidil. Hydralazine is the DOC for hypertensive emergency in pregnancy while diazoxide is DOC for **hypoglycaemia** caused by insulinoma. Minoxidil is the **DOC** for male pattern baldness and is often used with **finasteride.** The latter acts by inhibiting the conversion of testosterone to dehydrotestosterone by blocking the enzyme 5-alpha reductase.
- DOC for **hypertension** with **diabetes/nephropathy** or normal rennin hypertension is **ACE inhibitors.**
- MC side effect-cough, also cause hyperkalemia, contraindicated in bilateral renal artery stenosis. Their most common side effect is dry cough (reduced by aspirin). Cough is *bradykinin* mediated. These include hyperkalemia, angiodedema and

proteinuria. Hypotension occurs and is mediated by ACE inhibition.

- All ACE inhibitors except lisinopril and captopril are prodrugs; all except moexipril and fosinoril should be avoided in renal failure; particularly when levels of creatinine is more than 2.5 mg/dl.
- Losartan can safely be used in renal failure.
- **ACE-inhibitors** are now **DOC for CHF;** but they don't increase cardiac output. They reduce preload, afterload and increase renal blood flow.
- They are also the DOC for unilateral renal artery stenosis, diabetes with hypertension, diabetic nephropathy and nephropathy with hypertension.
- They are **contraindicated** in pregnancy (because of fetopathy), bilateral renal artery stenosis, HOCM and renal failure.
- **Sodium nitroprusside** is the fastest and shortest acting anti-hypertensive drug (arterial and venodilator). It acts by stimulating cGMP (mechanism similar to nitrates). It is DOC for **hypertensive emergencies** and is used for producing hypotensive anesthesia (isoflurane is an alternative). It gets metabolized to **thiocyanate** (accumulation occurs) and is safe in IHD.

- **Alpha-methyldopa** and clonidine are alpha-2 agonists acting by reducing adrenergic discharge from presynaptic neurons. *These act by reducing cardiac output, peripheral resistance or both.* **Guanfacine** and **guanabenz** are other alpha-2 agonists. **Guanethidine** and **Guanadrel**, work as complex ganglion blockers and guanethidine is used in reflex sympathetic dystrophy, thyroid opthalmopathy and to produce **"pharmacological sympathectomy".**

- Most common side effects of methyldopa (DOC for HTN in pregnancy) and clonidine are sedation and dry mouth. Former can cause autoimmune hemolytic anaemia **(Coomb's positive)** and hepatitis.

- Discontinuation of clonidine causes rebound hypertension due to increase in sympathetic activity.

- Clonidine is DOC for **diabetic diarrhoea** and is used to reduce hyperactivity due to opioid withdrawal. It also reduces renal vascular resistance. Hence, does not increase rennin release.

- **Nifedpine** is vasodilator calcium channel blocker, however it is not used now a days as it causes reflex -tachycardia. It is however the drug of choice for peripheral vascular disease. **Nimodipine** is DOC for subarachnoid hemorrhage, while nicardipine is **cardioselective** calcium channel blocker.

- CCBs are lipid, electrolyte, uric acid, glucose and lipid neutral drugs.
- **Amlodipine** is safest, longest and most efficacious calcium channel blocker. It has least incidence of hypotension, bradycardia and constipation. Hence it is most commonly used CCB.

ANTIARRHYTHMIC DRUGS

- Arrhythmia are rhythm disturbances of heart accompanied by too fast or to slow heart rate. **Vaughan Williams** divided them into four types and **Singh** added fifth category.
- **Class 1a** increase ERP; class 1b decrease ERP while 1c have no effect on ERP. **Amiodarone shares the effects of class 1a on electrophysiology.** It mainly includes QT prolongation and increase in APD.
- **Quinidine** can increase plasma levels of digoxin mainly by reducing renal clearance of digoxin. Drug also displaces digoxin but that is minor a mechanism.
- It has anticholinergic activity (paradoxical tachycardia occurs). For treating this tachycardia, digoxin, a drug with cholinergic activity is used. This could result into a drug interaction. Therefore, dose of digoxin should be reduced when used along with digoxin.
- Quinidine cause **thrombocytopenia** and is the most common drug causing QT interval prolongation. Its most common drug interaction occurs with **digoxin** (reduces renal clearance) hence can cause toxicity.

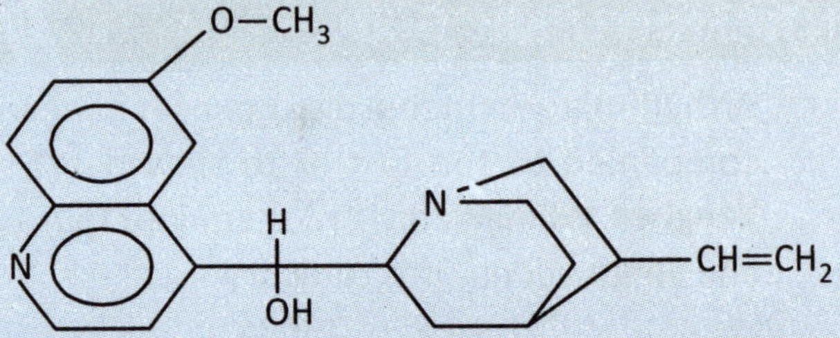

Figure: *Quinidine*

- **Procainamide** is most common drug causing drug induced SLE (kidney is NOT involved); it is used in ventricular arrhythmia refractory to lidocaine.
- It undergoes acetylation (Other drugs undergoing acetylation are: INH, hydralazine (acts by releasing nitric oxide like nitrates), dapsone, sulphonamides, caffeine, PAS).
- **Disopyramide** has maximum anti-cholinergic property. Therefore, it is avoided in elderly patients.
- Lidocaine is least cardio-toxic drug and it reduces ERP; it is DOC for ventricular tachycardia and fibrillation. In high dose, it can exhibit neurotoxic effect (seizures).
- Phenytoin is used for **digoxin-induced arrhythmia;** however DOC is lidocaine. This is because it causes hypotension and tachycardia upon IV injection.

- **Amiodarone** is the most efficacious, broadest spectrum and longest–acting (t½ = 70-100 days) anti-arrhythmic drug. Its most common side effect is pulmonary fibrosis-it also causes hypothyroidism and hyperthyroidism (it contains iodine in its structure). **Skin pigmentation** occurs. QT and ERP prolongation are seen but does not produce *torsade de pointes.* It is used for maintenance of sinus rhythm in atrial flutter and fibrillation. **Ibutilide** and **dofetilide** are DOCs for acute attack of flutter/fibrillation.

- **Bretylium** is DOC for LA induced arrhythmia-acts by inhibiting release of norepinephrine (**Bupivacaine** is the most common LA causing cardio-toxicity). It should not be combined with TCADs as both the drugs have mutually opposite mechanism of action.

- **Sotalol** is beta-blocker with K^+ channel blocking activity. It prolongs QT interval-most common drug prolonging QT interval is however quinidine. It increases plasma levels of digoxin by reducing renal clearance.

- **Adenosine** is the **shortest** acting anti-arrhythmic drug (<10 seconds) and is **DOC** for paroxysmal supraventricular tachycardia. Its most common side effect is flushing. Verapamil and diltiazem are the alternatives. Vagal stimulating maneuvers are helpful in the treatment.

- **Torsade de pointes** is the most common drug induced arrhythmia and quinidine is most common drug causing it. It is of two types: congenital and acquired. Former is treated by beta-blockers while latter by isoproterenol. **Magnesium** is used for acute attack, while pacemaker is the long-term solution.
- **Digoxin** is an antiarrhythmic drug used in selected cases with supraventricular arrhythmia. It works by reducing the conduction through AV node.

CONGESTIVE CARDIAC FAILURE (CHF)

- CHF means insufficient cardiac output. It leads to reduced blood flow and hence leads to release of rennin. This stimulates aldosterone, which leads to accumulation of sodium and water.
- Release of angiotensin-II leads to increase in preload and after load due to veno and arterial constriction (increased pre and after load).
- Digoxin is the most commonly used cardiac glycoside that increases cardiac output due to inhibition Na^+K^+ ATPase. Important pharmacological effect of digoxin is to increase cardiac output and decreases heart rate due to vagal stimulation. Electrophysiologically, it increases ERP of AV node, while reduces the ERP of ventricles, atria and ectopic pace makers.
- Digoxin ($t_{½}$ = 24-36 h) is excreted **unchanged** from kidney. Therefore, it is **contraindicated in renal failure. Digitoxin** ($t_{½}$ = 165 h) undergoes elimination by bile and hence is safe in renal failure (CI in hepatic failure). Cardiac glycosides have large volume of distribution and hence haemodialysis is **ineffective** in digoxin poisoning.
- Digoxin acts by **inhibiting Na+K+ATPase** and therefore increases cardiac contractility; heart rate is NOT increased (rather, decreased due to

AV block). It stimulates ectopic pacemakers therefore, causes cardiac arrhythmia.

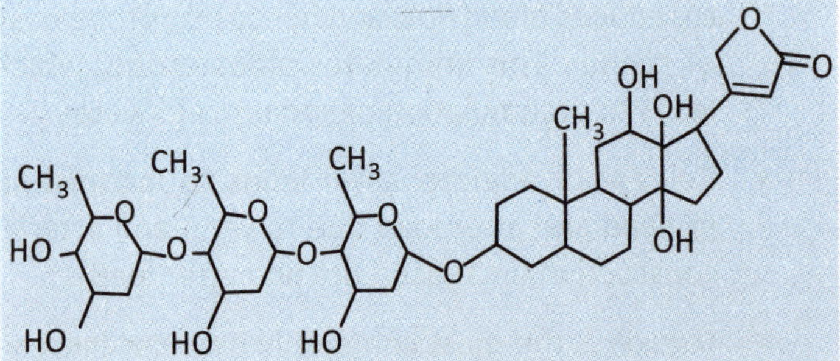

Figure: *Digoxin*

Table: Contraindications of digoxin

- Obstructive cardiomyopathy (Cardiac output can not increase)
- Ventricular tachycardia (do not try cardioversion in digoxin induced arrhythmia as VT gets converted into ventricular fibrillation)
- Partial heart block (it is safe in full heart block)
- Cardiac tamponade (mechanical obstruction occurs)
- High output failure (Cardiac output is already increased)
- Constrictive pericarditis (mechanical obstruction occurs)
- Renal failure (elimination is by renal route)
- Myocarditis* (Response is unpredictable)
- Myxedema* (Clearance is reduced)
- Thyrotoxicosis* (Response is exaggerated)

*Cautious use is indicated

- Most common precipitating factor of digoxin toxicity is hypokalemia (hyperkalemia is protective). Thiazides are most common drugs that produce hypokalemia. Importantly, these drugs are used along with digoxin for their fluid clearing action.

Table: Factors precipitating digoxin toxicity

- Metoclopramide (increase motility, increased absorption)
- Quindine (reduce clearance)
- Thiazides use (hypokalemia facilitates digoxin binding to heart)
- Hypercalcemia (synergistic cardiotonic actions)
- Hypomagnesemia (increased excitability of heart)

- DOC for **digoxin toxicity** is potassium (CI in overdose); hyperkalemia is a protective factor in digoxin overdose.
- DOC for overdose of digoxin toxicity is **DIGIBIND** (Fab fragment of digoxin binding antibody). Haemodialysis is ineffective. This is because, the drug gets concentrated in the heart as well skeletal muscle and there is therefore no use of filtering the blood.
- BLAST (**B**arbiturates, **L**ithium, **A**lcohols and **S**alicylates) are drugs/chemicals where

haemodialysis is the treatment of choice in case of poisoning caused by these drugs.

- ACE inhibitors are DOCs for CHF. These are veno and arterial dilators and also increase renal blood flow. They therefore reduce preload, after load and increase renal blood flow and hence cause diuresis as well.

HYPOLIPIDEMIC DRUGS

- **Statins** are most commonly used hypolipidemic drugs. They act by inhibiting HMG CoA reductase which is the key enzyme responsible for biosynthesis of cholesterol. Since they inhibit cholesterol biosynthesis in liver, therefore, their use is accompanied by **compensatory** rise of LDL receptors on liver (also seen with bile acid binders). Most common side effect of statins is myopathy. Some patients have hepatitis. Rarely myoglobinuria can occur.

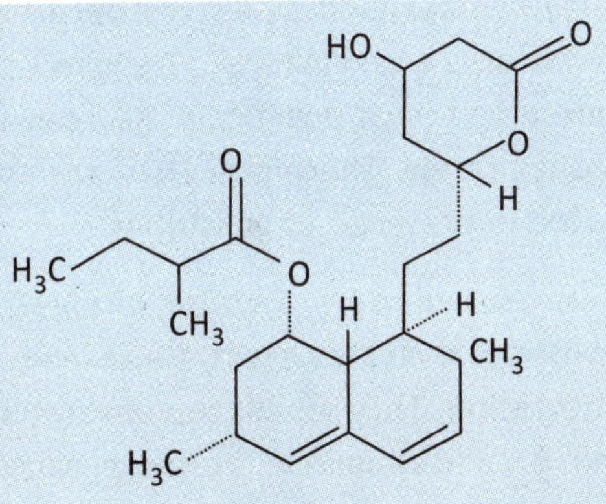

Figure: ***Lovastatin***

- Both lovastatin and simvastatin are prodrugs. Metabolism of statins is inhibited by erythromycin or any other enzyme inhibitors can cause accentuation of myopathy. Increase risk of muscle injury can also occur with clofibrate given alone or with lovastatin.

- Fibric acid derivatives include clofibrate, fenofibrate, and gemfibrozil. These act by activating **PPRAP**-gamma (peroxisome proliferator receptor activated protein gamma). They act by inhibiting hydrolysis of TAG; hence reduce TAG levels. Fibrates are DOC for triglycerdemias. Niacin is an alternative. Avoid in patients with gall stones.
- They increase good cholesterol but do not reduce levels of LDL cholesterol. Their most common side effect is GI upset but they can form gallstones rarely. Therefore, they are **contraindicated** in presence of gallstones.
- Bile acid binders include **cholestyramine, colistipol and colesvelam.** These inhibit bile acid absorption. They inhibit the absorption of vitamin B_{12} and vitamin K; therefore, cause megaloblastic anemia and increased risk of bleeding. Cholestyramine reduces oral absorption of OCPs, digoxin and tolbutamide.
- **Nicotinic acid** increase t-PA levels, sugar, uric acid and reduce fibrinogen. It is however poorly

tolerated. Flushing is its most common side effect; can be reduced by using aspirin. It is contraindicated in gout, diabetes and peptic ulcers.

- It is the only drug increasing HLD levels to clinically significant levels, hence is DOC for increasing HDL levels.

Unit 4

Renal Drugs

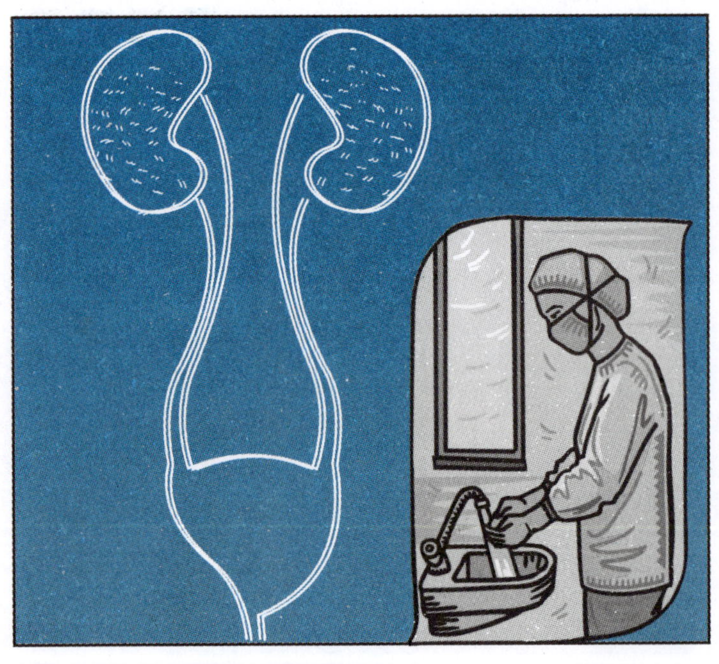

Let the evil go and good retained.

—Author

- Diuretics are drugs increasing urine formation while antidiuretics are drugs that reduce urine formation.
- Thiazides (Act on DCT) are DOC for **hypertension** as they act slowly and conserve calcium (useful in osteoporosis) diabetes insipidus of nephrogenic type (most commonly used drug is hydrochlorothiazide), **Liddle's syndrome, idiopathic hypercalciuria and hypercalcemia in hyperparathyroidism.**
- **Hydrochlorothiazide** is most commonly used except metolazone and indapamide (undergo biliary elimination) are unsafe in renal failure. Other thiazides are safe in renal failure up to glomerular filtration rate 35 ml/min. Most common side effect is hypokalemia and can impair glucose tolerance as they interfere with conversion of proinsulin to insulin.

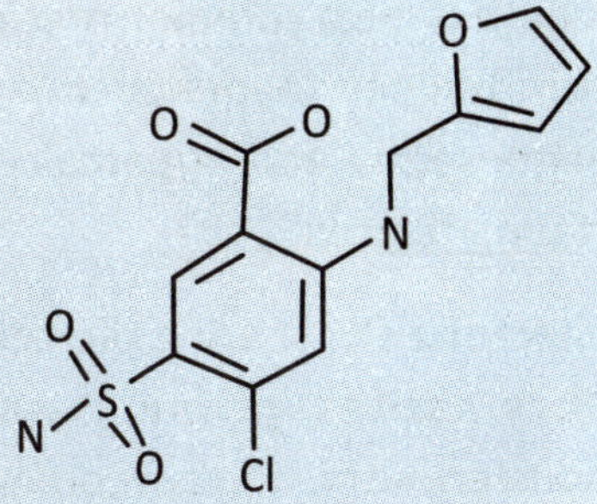

Figure: ***Furosemide***

- **Furosemide** (Acts on *Loop of Hanle*) is the **fastest** acting and **most efficacious** diuretics (also called **high-ceiling** diuretic). They are DOC for edema with renal failure, hypercalcemia and acute hyperuricemia. On acute use, they reduce uric acid levels due to uricosuric action, while on chronic administration they too increase levels of uric acid.

- Both loop diuretics and thiazides share common side effects. For example, most common side effect of both thiazides and furosemide is hypokalemia. Both of them are well absorbed orally. They however have different site of action and differ on many side effects as well. For example, furosemide causes hypocalcemia and hypouracemia on acute use. Additionally, furosemide is ototoxic, while thiazide is free from ototoxicity.

- Hypokalemia is most common precipitating factor of digoxin toxicity (hyperkalemia prevents it). Hypomagnesemia and hypercalcemia also are precipitating factors.

- **Spironolactone** (K^+ sparing diuretic) is DOC for refractory ascites, primary and secondary hyperaldosteronism. Its most common side effect is hyperkalemia-*do not use it with K^+ or with ACE inhibitors*. It can cause gynaecomastia. **Eplerenone** is newer aldosterone antagonist free from gynecomastia causing potential. It also causes hyperkalemia. Both act on collecting duct. Eplerenone is used as an antihypertensive drug.

- **Amiloride, triamterene** are other K^+ sparing diuretics and act by blocking sodium channels. They can cause hyperuricemia and reversible azotemia. They act on late distal tubule and early collecting duct.

- **Acetazolamide** (carbonic anhydrase inhibitor) is the weakest of all diuretics; they cause inhibition of bicarbonate reabsorption and hence cause metabolic acidosis. Common side effects are **allergic** rashes followed by paraesthesia. **Dorzolamide** is used topically in glaucoma. **Acetazolamide (DIMOX)** is used in *narrow angle glaucoma, acute mountain sickness, partial epilepsy* and *familial periodic paralysis.* Drug is avoided in liver cirrhosis.

- **Mannitol** is osmotic diuretic and causes hyperkalemia, hypovolemia and pulmonary edema. This is because it can cause expansion of plasma volume as it is freely filtrated.

- It is the **DOC** for brain edema (not in intracerebral hemorrhage), *acute narrow angle glaucoma,* anticancer drug induced nephrotoxicity and oligouric renal failure. It is contraindicated in *pulmonary edema, intracerebral hemorrhage* and anuria.
- Demeclocycline and lithium are **ADH receptor antagonists,** used in syndrome of inappropriate ADH secretion (also called as antidiuretic). They can cause **nephrogenic diabetes insipidous** as a side effect.
- Demeclocycline, a long-acting tetracycline antibiotic is the **DOC** for SIADH; lithium is an alternative.

Unit 5

Drugs for Central Nervous System Diseases

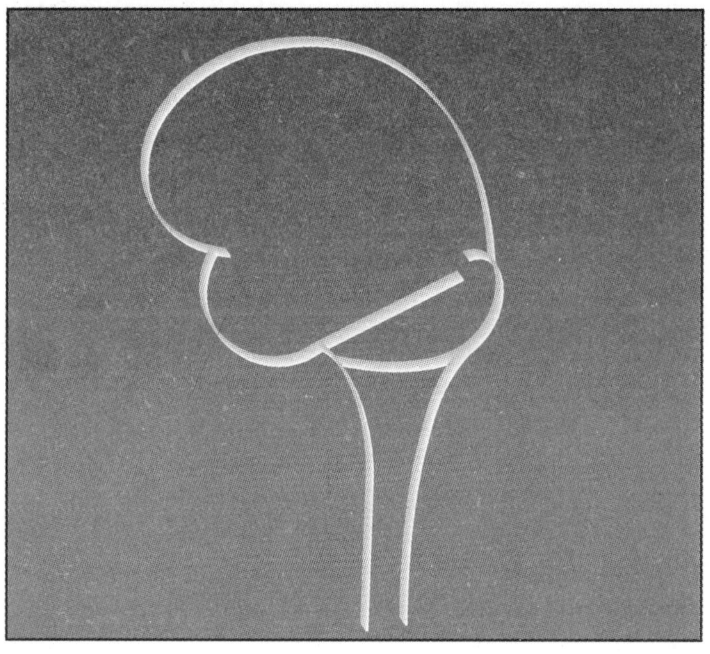

Communication is our connection to the world.

—Kris King, Wings Seminars

SEDATIVE HYPNOTICS

- Sedative is a drug that brings calmness while hypnotics produce sleep. Benzodiazepines are most commonly used sedative hypnotics.

- Benzodiazepines are lipid-soluble drugs and are well absorbed but have high first pass metabolism. They penetrate blood brain barrier well and form active metabolites. They, however, do not participate in cytochromal enzyme mediated drug interactions. That means, they neither induce or inhibit the enzymes. This is opposed to phenobarbitone that is the most potent enzyme inducer. It can cause clotting when given with warfarin. Chloral hydrate can displace warfarin from protein binding sites. This can lead to bleeding due to increase in levels of warfarin.

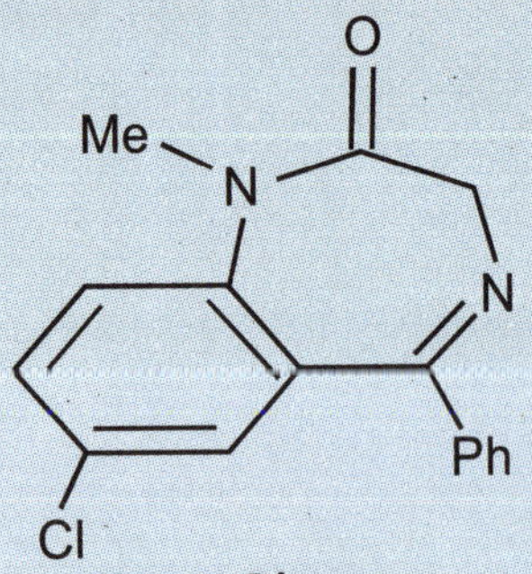

Figure: ***Diazepam***

- **Midazolam** is an ultra-short benzodiazepine used for sedation needed in short procedures like endoscopies.
- **Triazolam** is used for short-term relief of anxieties; due to short duration of action, it can cause daytime anxiety.
- **Diazepam** is among the most commonly used sedative and hypnotic with $t_{½}$-100 hours. Uses are given below:

Table: Uses of diazepam

- Febrile seizures (intra-rectal)
- Drug-induced hyperactivity
- Picrotoxin poisoning
- Prevention of seizures due to lidocaine
- Emergence delirium due to ketamine
- Drug-induced EPS
- Control of excitement in manic patients
- Tardive dyskinesia (clonazepam is an alternative)
- Alcoholic hallucinations.

- **LEO** (Lorazepam, Estazolam, Oxazepam) are water-soluble benzodiazepines. Lorazelam is DOC for status epileptics due to better safety and efficacy compared to diazepam. It can be given intramuscularly as opposed to diazepam. Lorazepam and oxazepam are metabolized outside liver. Hence are safe in liver diseases.

- Newer non-benzodiazepines for example **zopiclone**, **zolpidem** and **zaleplon** are safest hypnotics. They act upon *omega-1 receptors* (alpha subunit of $GABA_A$ receptors) and have less likelihood of tolerance and dependence.
- Benzodiazepines cause **anterograde** amnesia (head injury causes retrograde amnesia); lorazepam has maximum amnesia causing potential. **Flunitrazepam** causes amnesia and leads to loss of resistance in victim. Hence it is called as **"date rape drug".** It reduces the victim's resistance as the drug produces muscle relaxation.
- **Chlordiazepoxide** (high dose) is DOC for alcohol withdrawal from alcohol. Clonazepam, clorazepate and clobazem are used as anticonvulsant. Due to development of sedation and tolerance, they are NOT used commonly. However, they can be added if the primary anticonvulsant are ineffective.
- **Gama hydroxybutyrate** is a tasteless liquid and is used elicitly as 'date rape drug' or a 'party drug' or 'club drug'.

- **Ramelteon** is a newer hypnotic and is melatonin receptor agonist. This has been licenced for use in initial insomnia.
- **Buspirone** (5-HT_{1A} agonist) is a non-sedative anxiolytic drug that is devoid of properties possessed by diazepam such as muscular relaxation, amnesia, sedation, anti-convulsant action etc. Its main **drawback** is that it takes two weeks to start its anti-anxiety action. Therefore, is used in maintenance of patients with generalized anxiety disorders rather than in acute phase. It is free from tolerance and abuse potential.
- **Flumazenil** is the antidote of benzodiazepine receptors; it is short-acting drug (1 hour) and has to be repeated many times. It is also effective in hepatic coma. Main drawback is **respiratory depression.** This occurs due to short duration of action of drug. It is ineffective in overdose caused by other CNS depressants like TCADs, opioids and alcohol.

ANTI EPILEPTIC DRUGS

- Epilepsy is recurrent convulsive disorder. It occurs due to increase in glutamate and decrease in GABA content.
- Phenytoin acts by inhibiting **depolarizing shift** in neurons; most side effect is gum hyperplasia (maintain oro-dental hygiene).

Table: Side effects of phenytoin

- Hirsutism (avoid in young woman)
- Hypocalcemia (decrease in calcium absor-ption)
- Osteomalacia (may give with calcium and vitamin D)
- Megaloblastic anemia (occurs due to decreased folic acid absorption-do **MCV** testing; MCV > than 90 f/litre indicates megaloblastic anemia)
- **Pseudolymphoma** (resembles Hodgkin's lymphoma)
- Hypersensitivity **(discontinue the drug)**

- It is important to note that only absolute indication of phenytoin is hypersensitivity; rest of the problems can be managed by dosage adjustments.
- IV injection causes hypotension and tachycardia; respiratory arrest and arrhythmia are rare complications. **(Fos) phenytoin,** a water-soluble analogue

of phenytoin is free from these problems and can be given intramuscularly. It also does not cause 'red-glove syndrome' that occurs due to leakage of phenytoin leading to erythema and swelling.

- **Carbamazepine** is DOC for all kind of neuralgias (trigeminal\glossopharyngeal) and partial seizures; most common side effect is rash (10%), and others include leukopenia and hepatitis. It also causes SIADH.
- **Gabapentin** is fast emerging as the DOC for neuralgias. Oxcarbazine is a newer keto analogue, less potent than carbamazepine. It undergoes **autoinduction** and forms an active metabolite (epoxide); which is responsible for side effects. Pregabalin is a newer anti-neuralgia drug.
- **Valproic acid** is broadest spectrum anti-epileptic drug.

Table: Uses of valproic* acid

- GTCS
- Akinetic seizures
- Atonic seizures
- Myclonic epilepsy
- Mixed epilepsies

*It is now preferred as the drug of choice for absence seizures also due to its better efficacy. Studies indicate that it has the potential to become first line drug in mania and prophylaxis of migraine also.

- It may causes hepatotoxicity mainly in children, weight gain, and alopecia. It is a GABAergic drug (increase GABA release); **vigabatrine** is another such drug but it inhibits **GABA transaminase enzyme.**
- **Phenobarbitone**, the most commonly used barbiturate and is contraindicated in acute intermittent porphyria. It is DOC for hemolytic anemia, jaundice in newborn, and epilepsy following febrile seizures. In overdose, **hemodialysis** should be done; there is no **antidote**.
- **Ethosuccimide** is the DOC for absence seizures. It acts by inhibiting T-currents in thalamus and causes GI upset. Rarely, leukopenia also occur. It is important to know that in complicated absence seizures; sodium valproate is preferred.

Table: Newer antiepileptics

- Tiagabine (GABAergic drug)
- Topiramate (causes renal stones)
- Zonisamide
- Vigabatrine (Inhibits GABA-T enzyme)
- Levtiracetam (used in partial seizures)
- Lamotrigine (causes skin allergy, used in peripheral neuropathies and as an add on drug)
- Gabapentin (GABA analogue); inhibits GABA uptake.

ANTIPARKINSON DRUGS

- **Levodopa** is most effective anti-Parkinson drug and is the only drug that lowers mortality in Parkinson's disease. It is a pro-drug with low bioavailability due to high first pass metabolism. Early side effects include nausea, vomiting, postural hypotension and hallucinations. Arrhythmia are rare and occur due to peripheral conversion of levodopa into dopamine. Therefore, levodopa is given with carbidopa (combination is available as 1:4 or 1:10 and is known as **SINEMET**. Main advantage of SINEMET is less risk of peripheral side effects while main problem is high risk of hallucinations (more psychiatric side effects). Risk and motor fluctuations however remains same.

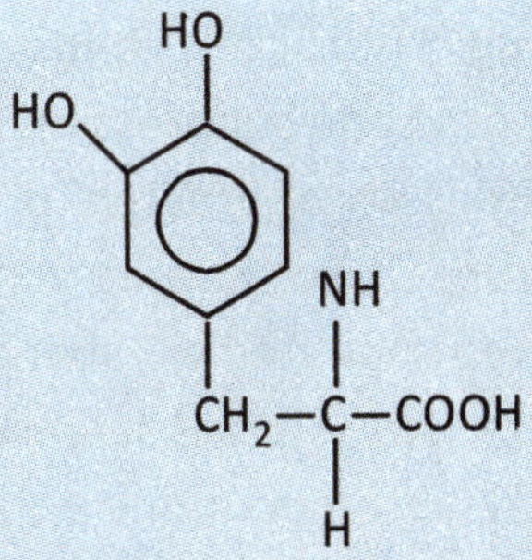

HO
HO
NH
CH_2—C—COOH
H

Figure: *Levodopa*

- **Amantidine** (also an antiviral drug used mainly for prophylaxis of Influenza A2) enhances dopamine transmission. Its most common side effect is ankle edema (Rx: Diuretics) and is contraindicated in renal failure and epilepsy. It also causes livido-reticularis. Amantadine can be used for motor fluctuations produced by levodopa.
- Pergolide, *piribidl* are dopamine D1 receptor agonists used in early stages of disease. *Ropiniole* (D2) and *pramipixole* (D3) agonists used in Parkinson disease. Their most common side effect is excessive sedation **"sleep attacks". However, they have less risk of motor fluctuations.**
- **Apomorphine, a D1 partial agonist** is used for so called episodes of hypomotility (freezing episodes).
- **Bromocriptine** is D2 **partial agonist** and is DOC for drug induced hyperprolactinemia, prolactinoma and suppression of unwanted lactation (**B6** is an alternative drug). It is a short acting drug, causes nausea vomiting and needs to be given repeatedly; cabergoline is a longer acting alternative and is safer during pregnancy. Now a days, bromocriptine is a new drug for diabetes.

- **Pergolide** is a D1 partial agonist and is more potent and longer acting than bromocriptine.
- Tolcapone and entacapone are **COMT inhibitors** used as **'add on'** drugs and are also useful in advanced Parkinson disease patients. Tolcapone is hepatotoxic while entacapone should be avoided in renal failure.
- **Triheyphenidyl (Pacitane/Benzhexol)** is the DOC for drug induced Parkinson's disease. Levodopa is ineffective as there is no dopamine deficiency. Though, L-dopa affects all manifestations but mainly affects bradykinesia; trihexyphenydyl affects rigidity.

OPIOIDS

- **Morphine** was isolated by Serturner (1807) from poppy plant it is analgesic and anti-tussive.

Table: Mu receptors actions

• Analgesia	• Euphoria
• Nausea	• Vomiting
• Respiratory depression	
• Cough suppression	
• Meiosis	• Constipation

- Tolerance to meiosis and constipation does not develop. Pentazocine, nelbuphine and butorphanol are kappa agonists. These drugs can have **psychomimetic** effects. *Kappa* mainly mediate spinal analesgia while dysphoria is due to activation of delta receptors.
- Opioids act by G protein coupled receptors, which lead to cellular hyperpolarization and inhibition. They reduce release of substance P. All opioid receptors (mu, kappa, and dela) mediate spinal and supra-spinal analgesia).

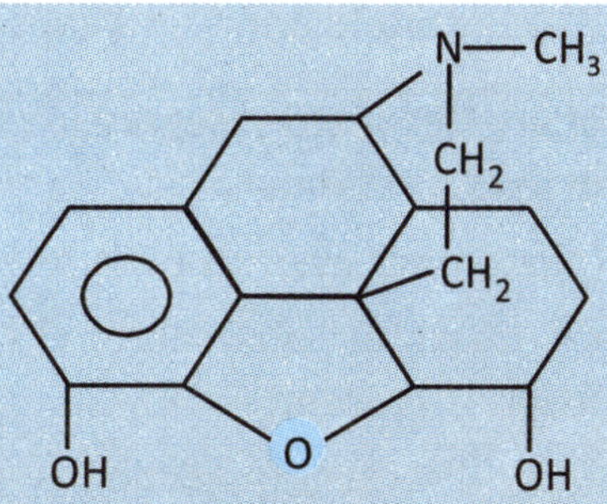

$$\text{Morphine structure: } N\text{—}CH_3,\ CH_2,\ CH_2,\ OH,\ O,\ OH$$

Figure: **Morphine**

- **Morphine**, the main alkaloid obtained from Papaver Somniferum (dose 0.1 = 0.2 mg/kg) and is the DOC for patient controlled analgesia (epidural), left ventricular failure with pulmonary edema, cancer pain (oral), pain of terminal illness, patient controlled analgesia and pain of acute myocardial infraction.
- 1/100th dose is effective if given intrathecally. Sufentanyl is only opioid that requires higher dose than oral in case of epidural.
- Epidural morphine can cause delayed respiratory depression. Morphine should be avoided in children. Remifentanil is the shortest acting opioid and alfentanil and sufentanil are maximally protein bound opioids.

Table: Opioid contraindications

- Head injury (respiratory depression can increase ICT due to CO_2 retention)
- BPH (Anatomical obstruction is present)
- Acute intestinal obstruction (Anatomical obstruction is present)
- Personality disorders (Addiction is more likely)
- Severe bronchial asthma (Bronchoconstriction occurs)
- Billary colic (Colic can be precipitated)
- Renal colic (Spasm of ureter can occur)
- Hypovolemia (Hypotension gets exaggerated due to hypotensive action)

- Pethidine is synthetic opioid that has **anticholinergic property** (causes mydriasis) while other opioids cause meiosis. It has no cough suppression activity, is less potent than morphine, safe in billary and renal colic and causes tachycardia. Therefore, pethidine and pentazocine should be avoided in pain of AMI. It should be avoided in cancer pain due to its brief duration. It is used in obstetrics for its analgesic action.
- **Pethidine** gets accumulated in renal failure causing hyperreflexia; this is known as norpethidine syndrome. It is therefore, **contraindicated** in

anuria. This can also occur when the drug is either used in high doses or for prolonged periods. Constipation is less with pethidine.

- Buprenorphine is the **longest** acting opioid ($t_{1/2}$ = 8 hours) that has alcohol anti-craving properties (methadone is DOC for opioid detoxification.
- **Naloxone** is the DOC for opioid overdose but doesn't reverse the overdose of buprenorphine due to its ceiling effect. Side effects do not include pulmonary edema.
- Buprenorphine is the longest acting opioid; **remafentanil** is the shortest acting opioid.
- Naltrexone is the **most potent opioid antagonist** and is used to reduce craving among opioid dependent and alcoholic patients. It is also a new anti-impotence drug.
- Opioids **do not have anti-inflammatory properties** but are useful in severe pain of visceral origin as they work by reducing the release of substance-P from substantia gelatinosa of spinal cord.
- Newer synthetic opioids (e.g., fentanyl, remafentanil, sufentanil, alfentanil) have high protein binding. Remafentanil and alfentanil have shortest onset of action time.

- **Sufentanil** is most potent opioid while naltrexone is most potent opioid antagonist (3-4 times more potent than naloxone).

- **Tramadol** is a *mu* receptor agonist that releases serotonin and inhibits norepinephrine uptake. It is useful in moderate pain (not intra-operatively-causes awareness) if NSAIDs and opioids are contra-indicated. Cautious use in epileptics and avoid in children.

- **Tapendol** is newer and safer version of tramadol.

- **Methadone** is drug of choice for opioid detoxification. **Acamproste** is used to reduce risk of relapse. **Clonidine** can be used to reduce opioid withdrawal induced autonomic hyperactivity.

AUTACOIDS

Histamine

- **Maximum amount of histamine** is found in lung mast cells (90% of body's histamine is present here). Other cells are basophils, and skin. High concentrations are found in hypothalamus. Intradermal injection causes **'triple response'** (RWF-redness, weal, flare-red wolf flying); meaning redness-vasodilation, flare respectively.

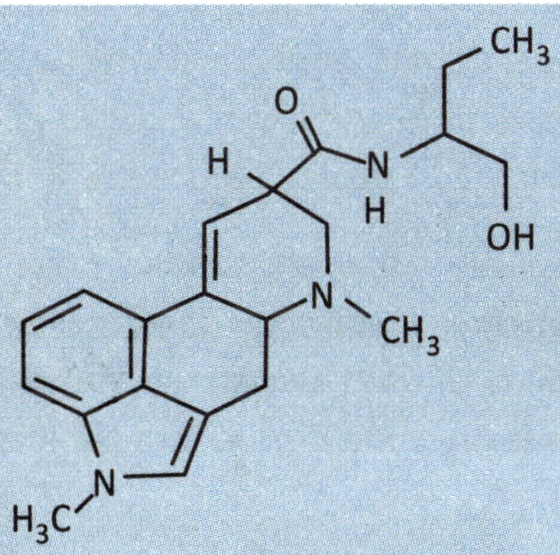

Figure: ***Histamine***

- Diphenhydramine and promethazine are antihistamines of older types with highest efficacy. Older agents are better for urticaria while the newer ones are better for common cold. Paracetamol can reduce the aches and pains associated with common cold.

- **Astemazole** is longest acting newer antihistamine and citirizine, although a member of newer non-sedative family; out of newer drugs it produces maximum sedation out of newer antihistamine. **Loratidine** produces least sedation. Older anti-histamines are better for urticaria and itching due to their anticholinergic effects while newer ones are better for sneezing and common cold etc.
- **Fexofenadine** (Allergra), a newer analogue of hepatotoxic and cardiotoxic drug named terfenadine and is not associated with *torsa de depointes.* Fexofenadine is the active metabolite of terfenadine.
- **Citirizine** is a metabolite of promethazine but is devoid of sedative effect at usual therapeutic doses (in some it produces sedation).
- **Promethazine** (Phenargan) is DOC for drug induced extra-pyramidal disturbances. It should be given as a slow intravenous injection.
- **Meclizine** and **cyclizine** are antihistamine drugs with **motion sickness.**

SEROTONIN

- Serotonin is known as **serum tonic.** It is a vasoconstrictor factor obtained from serum hence is known as so known as. Physiologically, it is an aggregator of platelets and vasoconstrictors. Role of serotonin in human allergic reactions is limited.
- **Sumatriptan**, a 5-$HT_{1b/1d}$ partial agonist is the DOC for acute attack of migraine; propranolol is DOC for prevention of migraine. It should not be combined with ergotamine and **should not be** given to patients with recent AMI. This is because; it can cause sudden coronary vasospasm.
- Sumatriptan can cause vasospasm, therefore is contraindicated in severe hypertension, angina and peripheral vascular disease patients.
- **Cyproheptadine** is the most common serotonin receptor blocker used clinically; methyserazide, ketotifen, ketanserine are other serotonin antagonists. They can rarely cause peritoneal fibrosis.

PROSTAGLANDINS (PGS)

- **Alprostadil** (PGE1) is used in infants to **maintain** the patency of ductus arterious before definite surgery can be done.
- **Carboprost** (15-methyl-PGF2_{α}) is the DOC for 2nd triamester abortion.
- **Dianaprost** (PGF2_{α}) tromethamine is used to produce abortion later than 15 weeks (intra-aminotic).
- **Misoprostol** (PGE_1 analogue) that is used for ulcer protection and conducting therapeutic abortions. Its **most common** side effect is diarrhoea (dose-dependent). That is why it is poorly tolerated. The drug is contraindicated in pregnancy.
- PGD_2 and PGE_2 are bronchodilator prostaglandins; rest of PGs have bronchoconstrictor properties.
- PGF2_{α} is a **vasoconstrictor** of pulmonary vessels, and is also used in post-partum hemorrhage and 2nd trimester abortions.
- PGF2_{α} (latanoprost) is the **DOC** for **low-tension glaucoma.** Most common side effect is iris pigmentation.

ALCOHOL

- Alcohol is most prevalent neurotoxin in our environment. It acts by **potentiating** the GABA.
- Disulfiram (metronidazole has disulfiram like effect) is alcohol dehydrogenase inhibitor and is the DOC for alcohol detoxification. **Cholordiazepoxide** is the DOC for alcohol withdrawal.
- It increases levels of TAG on chronic long-term consumption. Moderate consumption can however increase levels of HDL.
- It stimulates release of insulin and impairs glycogenolysis; hence can cause hypoglycemic response.
- Prolonged use can cause neuropathy and immune suppression.
- Legal limit of alcohol is up to 80 mg/dl in most nations and levels above 400 mg/dl are uniformly fatal; it follows zero-order kinetics. (Phenytoin, tolbuta-mide, theophylline, warfarin, aspirin, caffeine) also follow **zero-order** kinetics (fixed amount is metabolized per unit time). Alcohol is a water soluble chemical and its volume of distribution is equivalent to the total body water. Ethanol is eliminated at the rate of 10 mg/hour.

It is the amount of ethanol in one drink. All manifestations of alcoholism excluding amnesia can be reversed by using thiamine.

- Ethylene glycol poisoning shows presence of oxalate crystals in urine and tastes sweet. This poisoning is common in children. **Fomepizole/ethanol** are DOC for **methyl alcohol** poisoning (causes blindness due to optic atrophy) and ethylene glycol poisoning. Hemodialysis is indicated in case of severe intoxication. **Methanol,** also called as wood alcohol can produce severe damage to eyes and metabolic acidosis.

Unit 6

Non-Steroidal Anti-Inflammatory Drugs, Antigout and DMARDs

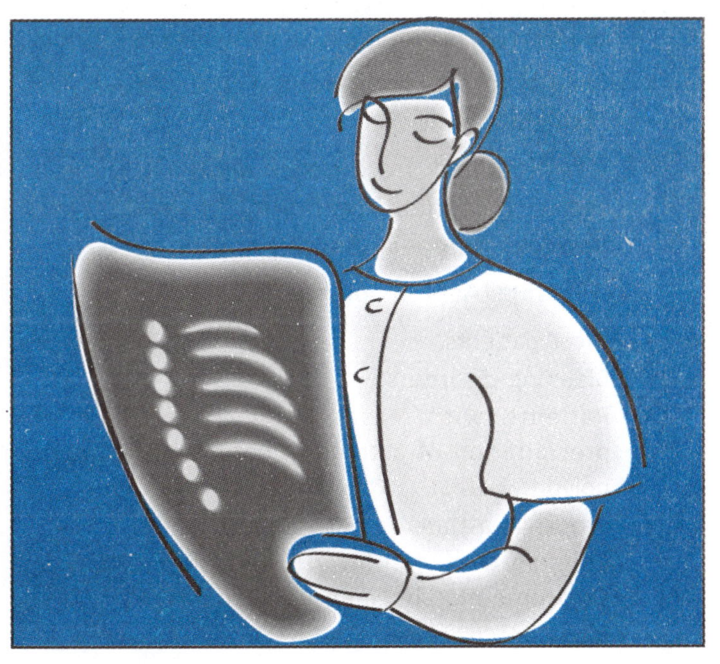

There is no evil without goodness.

—Costarican proverb, Central America

- **Aspirin** is most commonly used NSAIDs; it has analgesic, antipyretic, anti-inflammatory, anti-platelet and uricosuric actions (>3.5 gram/day). At dosages lower than 3.5 grams/day, it can cause retention of uric acid precipitating acute gout.
- Aspirin is **longest** acting anti-platelet drug acting for more than 72 hours; it's anti-platelet in low doses.
- In aspirin poisoning; metabolic acidosis is seen in children while metabolic alkalosis is seen in adults.
- Drug blocks cyclooxygenase in an irreversible covalent manner.
- Vitamin K and fresh frozen plasma are used in aspirin poisoning treatment. In severe cases, however, hemodialysis may have to used.

Table: Aspirin contraindications*

- Ulcer patients
- Bleeding disorders
- Patients with nasal polyp (Possibility of precipitation of asthma in patients with nasal polyp is 1-10%)
- Bronchial asthma

  Children with viral fever (Due to fear of Reye's syndrome-metabolic encephalopathy)
- Bleeding disorders

*In all patients where aspirin is contraindicated, **paracetamol** can be used. It is the most commonly used antipyretic with good analgesic property. It is **hepatotoxic** in overdose. Importantly, the manifestations appear after 24-48 hours. DOC for paracetamol toxicity is **N-acetyl cysteine**.

- Ibuprofen is safest older NSAID that causes **toxic amblyopia**. Aceclofenac has the potential to become NSAID of choice in the time to come.
- **Indomethacin** is a toxic NSAID. The drug was approved in 1963. Its a common side effect is frontal headache (50% cases); it is DOC for ankylosing spondylitits, acute gout, post-coital headache, Barter's syndrome and closure of PDA.
- The drug has antichemotactic action. Probenacid decreases renal clearance of indomethacin.
- Gastrointestinal upset is a common side effect. It also produces hyperkalemia, because of its ability to block renal prostaglandin synthesis. Edema and hypernatremia can also occur due to same reason.

Table: Indomethacin contraindications

- Drivers (produces confusion)
- Machinery operators
- Hematological diseases
- Neurological patients
- Psychiatrically ill patients
- Peptic ulcer patients

- **Sulindac** is a prodrug and undergoes enterohepatic circulation. It suppresses familial intestinal polyposis. This property seems to be independent of its ability to inhibit COX enzyme. It is also used as a tocolytic (recall that prostaglandins have oxytocic action. Therefore, NSAIDs, which are prostaglandin inhibitors will have opposite action).

- **Diclofenac** is most hepatotoxic NSAID; otherwise, NSAIDs do not cause liver damage. It is concentrated in joints hence quite useful for joint diseases.
- **COX-2 inhibitors** (Celecoxib, rofecoxib, valdecoxib, parecoxib etc.) are safer newer NSAID with less likelihood of symptomatic GI side effects such dyspepsia, ulcer and heartburn etc.
- Rofecoxib has recently been withdrawn because it can cause increased possibility of thrombo-emobolism.
- **H. pylori** is most common cause of peptic ulcers; NSAIDs are 2nd most common cause-NSAID induced ulcers are *H. pylori* negative. 'Triple therapy' (antibiotic, PPI and ulcer-healing drug combination) is used for eradication.
- **Probenacid** and **sulfinpyrazone** are uricosuric drugs. The latter also has a weak ant-platelet effect. Indomethacin does not interefere with uricosuric effect of probenacid and hence can be combined.

- **Ketorolac** is a NSAID and is also a *mu* agonist. The drug is used for postsurgical pain.
- **Allopurinol** (Xanthine oxidase inhibitor) is used in chronic gout, hyper-uricsemia due to anticancer drugs, urate nephropathy, and those with gout and renal failure.
- Allopurinol produces more rashes specially when given with ampicillin. It can cause retention of urate and precipitate an attack of acute gout.
- **Methotrexate** is most common used DMARD; hepatic fibrosis is the most common side effect; bone marrow suppression also occurs. It is DHFR inhibitor, anti-folate.

  Leuko-encephalopathy is a rare problem developing due to intra-thecal methotrexate.

  It is the DOC for ectopic pregnancy (actinomycin-D is an alternative), and CNS prophylaxis of leukemias. Leukovarin rescue (citrovorum factor) can reduce cytotoxicity.
- **Cyclosporine** (attacks CD4 cells), an immuno-suppresive drug is used as DMARD, causes hepato, nephrotoxicity but does not suppress bone marrow. It acts by inhibiting transcription of interleukins-2 by binding to calcineurine gene.
- Hypertension is its most common side effect and beta-blockers are DOCs for cyclosporin induced hypertension.

- **Tacrolimus** (PanGraf, VinGraf) is a newer immunosuppressive and binds to FKBP-12. The drug is comparatively potent than cyclosporine but has a comparatively higher risk of diabetes.

  Sirolimus (Rapamycin) is also a immuno-suppressive drug but does not bind to calcineurine. Side effect profile is same as that of cyclosporine.

- **Myocophenolate** is a prodrug and is converted into mycophenolic acid in the liver. The drug inhibits inosine monophosphate dehydrogenase. Bone marrow suppression is its most common side effect.

Unit 7

Antibiotics

Products of germs for cure of disease.

GENERAL INTRODUCTION

- Antibiotics are chemical substances derived from microorganisms and are fatal for them.
- They are of two main types: static and cidal

Table: Static and Cidal Antibiotics

Static
Chloramphenicol
Erythromycin
Aminoglycosides
Clindamycin
Linezolid
Lincomycin
Cidal
Beta-lactams
Vancomycin
Bacitracin
Cycloserine

- To achieve, static or cidal effect, antibiotics work by several mechanisms:

Table: Mechanism of Action of Antibiotics*

- **Protein synthesis inhibitors**
- Tetracyclins

*While antibiotics struggle to achieve these effects, bacteria become smarter and acquire resistance.

- Aminoglycosides
- Macrolides
- **DNA inhibitors**
- Rifampin
- **DNA damager**
- Metronidazole
- **Reverse transcriptase inhibitors**
- Zidovudine
- Lamivudine
- DNA repair mechanism inhibitors (DNA-Gyrase-2 inhibitors)
- Fluoroquinolones

Table: Mechanism of Resistance Among Pathogens

- Increased efflux
- Enzymes (e.g., beta-lactamases)
- Decreased permeability
- Mutation (e.g., methicillin)
- Plasmid mediated (e.g., chloramphenicol)

TETRACYCLINS AND CHLORAMPHENICOL

- All antibiotics acting by inhibiting protein synthesis other than tetracyclins act by inhibiting 50-S ribosomal inhibition. Tetracyclins act by inhibiting the attachment of t-RNA to 30-S of ribosome.
- Tetracycline are water-soluble antibiotics; hence are poorly absorbed by oral route. Food interferes with their absorption except in case of doxycycline, which is completely absorbed. Doxycycline and minocycline are lipid soluble and enter blood brain barrier.
- $FeSO_4$ and antacids reduce the absorption of tetracyclins but both $FeSO_4$ and tetracyclins can be given if their administration is separated by an hour or two. Both **doxycycline** and **minocycline** undergo elimination by bile, rest of tetracyclins are eliminated by kidneys. Hence both are safe in renal failure.
- Tetracyclins cause **deformities of bones and teeth** (maximum damage between, 3-6 years). Hence they are contraindicated in pregnancy, lactation and children below 8 years.

- Doxycycline causes **phototoxicity** while demeclocycline cause photosensitivity.
- Minocycline is used to **eradicate** the carriers of meningococcal meningitis along with rifampin.
- Tetracyclins are the DOC for (MRCP–**M**-mycoplasma, R-Ricketsiae, **C**-Chlamydia, **P**-prevention of plague). Other conditions are granuloma inguinale, lymphogranuloma venerum, and **Lyme's disease.**
- **Chloramphenicol** is a bacteriostatic antibiotic acting by inhibiting peptidyl transferase. It is cidal against *H. influenza.* It causes gray baby syndrome, which occurs due to defective glucoronidation–it, occurs in premature babies. Hence it should be avoided. It undergoes elimination by kidney; however drug dose is not much modified.
- It has anti-salmonella, anti *H. infleunza,* anti-rickeasiae and anti anerobic properties. It can be used for children with typhoid fever if culture and sensitivity report indicates that.

MACROLIDES

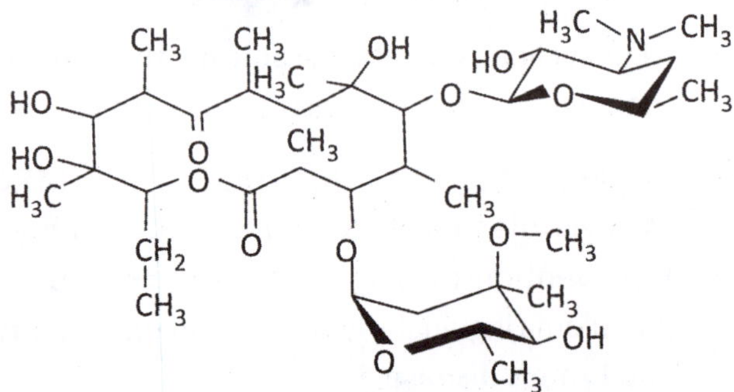

Figure: *Erythromycin*

- These are antibiotics with large rings (hence called macrolides).
- Macrolides act by inhibiting protein synthesis inhibiting 50-S of ribosome. They inhibit **initiation** of chain elongation.
- Erythromycin is most commonly used macrolides that causes diarrhea (stimulates **motilin** receptors) and hepatitis (more in pregnant women-specially estolate salt); acts on motilin receptors, increase intestinal motility.
- It is the DOC for whooping cough, diphtheria, chancnoids *complyobacter jejunii* infections.
- It is safer than erythromycin roxithromycin is longer acting and is more active against H. Influenza.

- Azithromycin is the **longest** acting macrolide; exhibits post antibiotic effect. It has excellent activity against *H. influenza.* It is DOC for trachoma and legionella.
- **Clindamycin** is the most common antibiotic causing *pseudomembranous enterocolitis.* It has excellent anti-anaerobic activity. Cephalosporins have emerged as prominent cause in recent years.

FLUOROQUINOLONES

- These are antibiotic with quinolone nucleus; they inhibit **DNA gyrase-II**-also called as topo-isomerase-IV. Development of resistance is rare.
- Nalidixic acid is the first quinolone but is only active against the gram-negative bacteria. Dose in renal failure should be reduced.
- They are well absorbed by oral route and have 100% bioavailaibility. Except, moxifloxacin, sparfloxacin and flurofloxacin dose should be reduced in renal failure.
- Fluroqunolones such as **ciprofloxacin** (has anti-pseudomonal activity) is one of the DOC for typhoid fever but damage growing cartilages; therefore are avoided in children <17 year age, pregnancy and lactation. It is the DOC for **eradiation** of carriers of typhoid fever.
- Gatifloxacin and sparfloxacin prolong QT interval and trofloxacin cause hepatitis-gatifloxacin also causes hypoglycemia.
- Levofloxacin and pefloxacin cause photosensitivity (Pefloxacin causes maximum photosensitivity).

SULPHONAMIDES

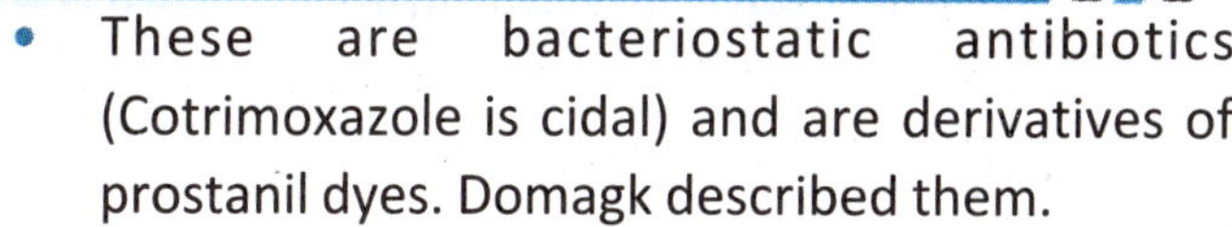

- These are bacteriostatic antibiotics (Cotrimoxazole is cidal) and are derivatives of prostanil dyes. Domagk described them.

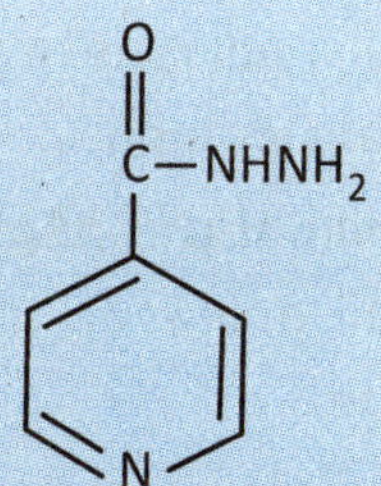

Figure: ***Sulfa nucleus***

- These are water-soluble, poorly enter blood brain barrier and undergo **acetylation.**
- Sulphonamides are **contraindicated** in newborns because they cause jaundice due to albumin displacement.
- **Cotrimoxazole** (Septran) act by sequential blockade, and is the DOC for **pneumocystic carnii**, Whipple's disease listeria and nocardiosis. **Sulpha allergy** is its most common side effect. It causes, megaloblastic anaemia, bone marrow suppression. Crystalluria is common hence liberal amount of water should be allowed.
- **Sulfacetamide** is used topically in trachoma (DOC for trachoma is azithromycin).

- **Silver Sulphadiazine** is the DOC for burns patients with *pseudomonas* colonization. Mefenide is an alternative drug but can produce hyperchloremia metabolic acidosis.
- **Spiramycin** is DOC for *Toxoplasmosis* in pregnancy; sulphadiazine+pyrimethamine is DOC in non-pregnant women.
- **5-aminosalicylic acid** (5-ASA) is DOC for inflammatory bowel disease. It is a prodrug of sulphasalazine.

BETA-LACTAM ANTIBIOTICS

- **Penicillins** and **cephalosporins** are two beta-lactam anitiotics containing 6-aminopenicilloic acid and 7-aminocephalosporinic acid.
- Beta-lactams are narrow spectrum antibiotics acting by inhibiting cell wall synthesis. They do so by binding to **PBP** (penicillin binding proteins) and inhibiting **transpeptidase**.
- Main mechanism of resistance is elaboration of penicillinases (beta-lactamases) in case of methicillin mechanism of resistance is mutation in peniclin biding proteins.

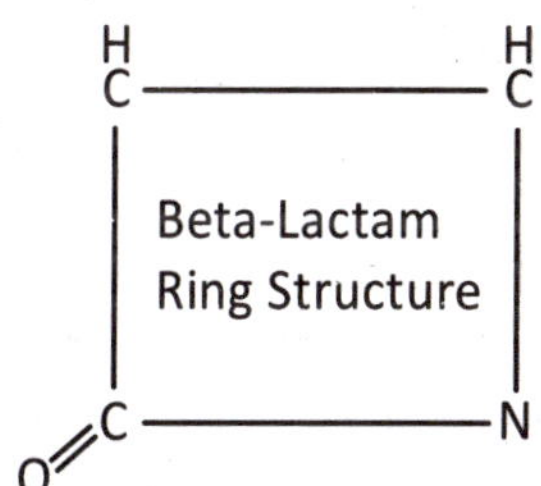

Figure: ***Beta-lactam ring***

- **Methicillin** causes interstitial nephritis, and is acid labile-it is used in staphylococcal infections. It is beta-lactamase stable. It is beta-lactamase stable and is used against staphylococci.

- All naturally occurring penicillins except **methoxy-penicllin** (peniclin V) are acid labile. It is acid stable and hence can be given orally. **Methicllin** is also acid labile. It is stable against beta-lactamases. Mechanism of resistance is mutation in peniclin binding proteins.
- Beta-lactams antibiotics are excreted unchanged by **tubular filtration**. Probenacid can be given to prolong their duration.
- Most common side effect of ampicillin is diarrhea (osmotic in origin); it also causes rashes (more common with allopurinol and in patients with infectious mononucleosis.
- **Ampicillin** is DOC for listeria meningitis and *enterococcus facalis.*
- **Amoxycillin** is DOC for otitis media and sinusitis.
- **Imipenem** (arbapenem) is the broadest spectrum antibiotic and is DOC for eneterobacter and broadest spectrum antibiotic of penicillin class.

  It is degraded in kidney by renal dehydropeptidase, which is inhibited by cilastin. **Meropenam** is free from this renal degradation effect.
- **Aztreonam** is aminoglycoside like antibiotic; it is even safer in patients with penicillin allergy. Seizures are rare side effects.

- **Oxacillin, nafcillin**, and **ampicillin** are other beta-lactams eliminated by bile. First two are anti-staphylococcal antibiotics and are stable against beta-lactamases.
- **Cefazolin** is the DOC for dirty and surgical wound prophylaxis. Cephalaxin and cefedroxil are two commonly used oral cephalosprins.
- **Cefuroxime** is 2nd generation cephalosporin that enters the blood brain barrier.
- **Cefoperazone, ceftazidime, ceftizoxime** are anti-pseudomonal cephalosporins. **Cefoperazone** causes thrombocytopenia while **ceftazidime** can cause neutropenia.
- **Ceftriaxone** (generation-3) is the **longest** acting cephalosporine and is DOC for *H. infleunza,* meningitis (except listeria), gonorrhea and typhoid fever. It is eliminated in bile, hence is safe in renal failure.
- **Cefoperazone** and **lorcarbacef** can cause disulphifram like reactions. **Moxalactam** is a third generation cephalosporin that can also cause thrombocytopenia.
- **Vancomycin** is DOC for MRSA, causes ototoxicity, nephrotoxicity, and its most common side effect is 'red man syndrome' (prevented by antihistaminics and glucocorticoids). It is past

DOC for pseudome-bransous enterocolitis. Current DOC is metronidazole due to better safety, cost and tolerability.

- **Teichoplanin** and **linezolid** can be used for VRSA (vancomycin resistant stahlycocus aureus), and VRE (vancomycin resistant enterococci). Linezoeid causes thrombocytopenia.
- **Streptogramins** (dalfopristin/quinapristin-1:4 combination). It is used for resistant gram-positive infections.

AMINOGLYCOSIDES

- Aminoglycosides cause **misreading** of t-RNA-amino acid complex and **premature termination** of chain elongation.
- These are bactericidal antibiotics and are synergistic with penicllins and cephalosporins
- Aminoglycosides are effective against gram-negative aerobic bacteria; they have no value against anaerobes. They exhibit **concentration dependent killing** effect upon bacteria.
- **Streptomycin** is the oldest aminoglycoside and is the DOC for plague tularemia and rhino-scleroma.
- **Gentamicin** is quite effective against **pseudomonas** and is most nephrotoxic aminoglycoside. It exhibits concentration dependent killing.
- Risk of nephrotoxicity is less when the drug is used as a single large dose rather than multiple doses. This is because, aminoglycosides exhibit concentration dependent killing.
- Amikacin is the **broadest** spectrum aminoglycoside and is **stable** in the presence of inactivating enzymes.

- Toberamycin is **antipsuedomonal aminoglycoside.**
- **Kanamycin, amikacin and capreomycin** are used in MDR tuberculosis.
- Netilmycin is **safest** aminoglycoside.
- **Neomycin** is the DOC for bowel sterilization in hepatic coma and before surgery. Lectulose is preferred now.
- **Aminoglycides** are narrow therapeutic antibiotics which share common toxicities viz. ototoxicity (auditory and vestibular), nephrotoxicity and neuromuscular blocking activity.

NH
N
NH_2
HO
HN
OH
H_2N
N
OH
O
O
O
H_3C
OH
O
HO
O
HO
NHMe
HO

Figure: ***Streptomycin***

- **Streptomycin** is most vestibulotoxic, while gentamicin is most nephrotoxic aminoglycoside.
- **Initial** manifestation of ototoxicity is loss of high frequency sound followed later by low frequency.
- Base of hair cells is first affected followed later by apex.
- Initial manifestation of vestibular toxicity (more common than auditory) is headache followed later by ataxia.
- **KAN** (kanamycin, amikacin and neomycin) are most auditory toxic aminoglycosides.
- Neomycin is most likely to lead to prolonged neuromuscular block.
- **Spectinomycin** is an aminoglycoside used in patients with allergy to penicillins having gonorrhoea.

ANTIFUNGAL DRUGS

- **Amphotericin-B** is DOC for invasive or systemic fungal infections; causes hypokalemia, nephrotoxicity and hypersensitivity (test dose is needed). Flucytosine, an antipyrimidine drug increases the penetration of Amp-B into cells. It is a prodrug that gets converted into 5-flurouracil.
- It is a photosensitive drug-protect from light. Nitroglycerine and sodium nitroprusside are other photosensitive drugs.
- It is the DOC for systemic fungal infections. Its liposomal formulation is used for leishmaniasis. Allopurinol, ketoconazole, miltifosine (most effective drug) are other antileishmiania drugs.
- **Itracnazole** is DOC for blastomycosis, blastomycosis and sporothrix and fluconazole for cryptococcal, meningitis (prophylaxis), coccidioidal and candida infections.
- **Griseofulvin** (inhibits microtubules) is DOC for systemic dermatophytoses, due to low efficacy, it has been replaced by terbinafine in onychomycosis. It is obtained from penicillium griseofulvum.

- It is a fungistatic drug that acts by inhibiting mitotic spindles, however, does not cause arrest of mitosis (Vincristine and colchicine produce metaphase arrest). It gets concentrated in *keratinocytes*. Its absorption is increased by fatty food and is reduced by phenobarbitone. Its most common side effect is headache. Its half-life is 24 hours. Disulfiram like reaction can occur.
- **Fluconazole** is used in 3Cs (coccidoidal mycosis, cryptococcal and candidal infections). In cryptococcal meningitis, it is used for prophylaxis and not treatment amphotericin B is preferred.
- **Terbinafine** is the DOC for onychomycosis; griseofulvin was used in past. It is not favored now a days due to low efficacy and high rate of relapse.
- Ketoconazole is the oldest antifungal drug with antiandrogenic and enzyme inhibiting properties. It follows zero order kinetics and can be hepatotoxic. The drug is anti androgenic.
- Ciclopirox, olamine, tolnaftate are weaker antifungals. Capsofungin is newer antifungal and is cidal.

ANTIVIRAL DRUGS

- **Acyclovir** is the DOC for all kind of *herpes* infections; its most common side effect is *nephrotoxicty*. Also causes neurotoxicity (e.g. seizures). Defective phosphorylation can produce *resistance*.

- **Ganciclovir is the DOC** for CMV infections and bone marrow suppression is its most common side effect.

- **Nevaripine+zidovudine** is used to reduce maternal to fetal transmission (risk is 30% with drugs and 2% without). **Nevirapine** is a prodrug. Drug resistance is a major problem. Reverse transcriptase inhibitors are used in combination and not alone.

- **Zidovudine+lamivudine** is used following accidental needle injury while drawing blood from HIV positive patient. Usually two drugs are sufficient, 3 drugs are needed in high-risk cases (duration of treatment is 4 weeks).

- Most common side effect of zidovudine is anaemia and mechanism of resistance is *mutation* in reverse transcriptase enzyme.

- **Lamivudine** (DOC for HBV) **does not cause neuropathy** while stavudine (MC drug), zalcitabine, diadanosine cause peripheral neuropathy. Entecavir is used in active, chronic and HBV with raised aminotransferase.
- **Adefovir** is an alternative drug useful in chronic hepatitis B infection. Tiprinavir is used in case of HBV infection resistant to several agents.
- Didanosine's most common side effect is **pancreatitis**, while zalcitabine's most common side effect is **peripheral neuropathy.**
- **HIV protease inhibitors** (Nelfinavir, squinavir, amprenavir, lopinavir, ritonavir and indinavir etc.) should not be used with rifampin. Their most common side effect is *lipodystrophy*. Indinavir can produce renal stone and hyperbillirubinemia. **Protease inhibitors** work by inhibiting the interaction between *Gag-Pol* gene which codes for enzymes which eventually make structural proteins.
- It is important to know that all the protease inhibitors are enzyme inhibitors. Therefore, giving them with other drugs can **increase** their plasma levels.
- **Ritonavir** is least likely to interact with rifampin hence can be given together. This is perheps

former is enzyme inhibitor while latter is an enzyme inducer. Indinavir causes renal stones.

- Tiprinavir is a newer HIV protease inhibitor useful even in patients resistant to other drugs of same class.
- **Rifabutin** can safely be used with HIV protease inhibitors as it is not as potent enzyme inducer compared to rifampin.
- **Amantadine** is antiviral used for prophylaxis of influenza A2 with anti-Parkinson activity. It acts by inhibiting viral assembly or release of virons.
- Ankle edema is its most common side effect and is contraindicated in epilepsy and renal failure. **Rimantadine** is more potent and longer acting. Ostelmavir and zanamavir are newer anti-viral drugs against H. influenza.
- Amantidine is useful for prophylaxis while ostelmavir is useful for treatment. Zanamavir is avoided in asthma.

ANTIMALARIALS

- Malaria is the most common cause of fever with chills and rigors. Sexual cycle takes place in mosquito while asexual cycle takes place in man.

Table: Chloroquine uses

- Prophylaxis of malaria
- Malaria in pregnancy
- P. Vivax malaria
- Sensitive falciparum malaria
- Tropical spleenomegaly.
- **Chloroquine** ($t_{½}$-50 hours) is long acting drug with cumulative potential. It acts by inhibiting hemoglobin utilization (it's a basic drug, raised pH of the vesicles). Its most common side effect is GI upset; prolonged use can cause optic neuritis (can interfere with blue color vision). Prolonged use can interfere with blue colour vision and average cumulative dose is 250 grams.
- Proguanil and pyrimethamine are slowly acting agents against erythrocytic forms of susceptible parasites. Proguanil is safe during pregnancy. *Clindamycin* is a slowly acting agent against the erythrocytic schizonts and is used with quinine and quinidine.

- *Fansidar* is a sulfadoxine and pyrimethamine combination and is used as a single dose for uncomplicated bacteria. It is not used for severe malaria as it is a slowly acting agent.
- However, when used with quinine, it can shorten the duration of action of quinine treatment.

  Importantly, Fansidar is not recommended for chemoprophylaxis.
- **Quinine** is a cinchona alkaloid and is DOC for severe falciparum malaria and cerebral malaria. Most common side effect is GI upset followed by hypoglycemia (occurs due to insulin release). Therefore, it is given along with 5% dextrose. Cinchonism (dizziness, tinitis etc.) can occur.
- It is the drug of choice for severe falciparum malaria. Quinine is gametocidal against all species except *plasmodium falciparum.*
- **Blackwater fever** occurs in partially treated patients with falciparum infections. It can cause renal failure. It reduces the release of acetylcholine and is used to treat nocturnal cramps.
- Pharmacokinetics of quinine varies in population but the drug does not develop toxicity in patients with malaria despite being given in high doses due to increased protein binding.

- Primaquine has **gemetocidal** (most efficient gamatocidal agent) activity and is the DOC for **eradication** of hypnozoites from liver.
- It's the most common drug causing hemolysis in G-6-P-D deficiency. It is used for reducing man to mosquito transmission of malaria.
- **Mefloquine** prolongs QT interval and is **contraindicated** in heart block, psychiatric and epileptic patients.
- It is most toxic antimalarial and is the DOC for chloroquine resistant malaria in pregnancy and in endemic area. Half life is about 30 days. Contraindications include: **PACE** (**P**sychiatric **P**atients, **A**rrythmias, **C**onduction disturbances, **E**pilepsy)
- **Sesquiterpine lactones derivatives** (artether, artemether artemisnin) are fastest acting anti-malarial drugs used in severe and resistant malaria. They do not prolong QT interval and are safe in patients with G-6-P-D deficiency.
- **Atovaquinone** is the new antimalarial used for **prevention** of malaria among travelers. It is also used in *pneumocyctis carnii*.

- Mefloquine can also be used but is neurotoxic. Doxycyline can be used in place of mefloquine. Atovaquinone is a long acting drug ($t_{½}$ = 2 days).
- Halofantrine and lumefantrine are **new antimalarials** causing QT prolongation. They are preferred for severe or multi-drug resistant cases.

ANTIAMEOBIC DRUGS

- Metronidazole acts by damaging DNA and is DOC for giardiasis, amoebiasis (hepatic and intestinal), *Trichomonas vaginalis and gardnerella vaginalis,* pseudomembranous enterocolitis. (MC –s/e nausea, metallic taste and disulfiram like reaction).
- It is contraindicated in first trimester of pregnancy. It kills the trophozoites but not the cysts of *E. histolytica.* Therefore, the drug should be combined with a luminal agent.
- **Tinidazole** is more potent, longer acting and is safer.
- **Satranidazole** is the safest nitroimidzole. It is devoid of nausea, vomiting and disulfiram like reaction.
- **Diloxanide furate** is DOC for asymptotic cyst passers; tetracyclins can be used for mild intestinal amoebiasis. **Puromomycin**, an aminoglycode is an alternative drug. Flatulence is the most common side effect.
- **Emetine/dehydroemetine** are used in serious cases with hepatic amoebiasis but are **cardiotoxic.** They are used in resistant cases and inhibit protein synthesis.

- **Idoquinol** is a weak antiameobic agent and is commonly used as an antidiarroheal agent. It also has good luminal activity. This drug has been known to produce subacute optic myeloneuropathy.

ANTITUBERCULAR DRUGS

- **INH** is most rapidly acting ATT acting by inhibiting mycoloic acid synthesis.

  It acts on both intra and extra-cellular bacteria-penetration into caseous material is best; peripheral neuropathy (prevented by B6) is most common side effect, also causes hepatitis.

- Rare side effects are leucopenia and "hand shoulder syndrome". Psychosis and seizures are rare problems. Transient amnesia has been reported. Agranulocytosis is rare. B6 is antidote of INH poisoning.
- It undergoes acetylation and is the DOC for prevention and treatment of tuberculosis latent tuberculosis.
- Rifampin is slowly acting ATT, acts on intermittent growers and spurters-can sterilize cavities, cause orange red coloration, inhibits DNA dependent RNA polymerase-causes hepatitis.
- It is also active against staphylococcus, meningococci, and legionella etc. It kills semidor-mant bacteria also.
- If given once a month or fortnightly, rifampin produces more s/e such as cutaneous syndrome,

abdominal syndrome, flu like syndrome. Reversible nephritis is a rare side effect. Light chain proteinuria and reversible nephritis are rare side effects.

- **Ethambutol** is only first line bacteriostatic drug, is not metabolized, excreted unchanged, causes interference of red-green (green more) vision (optic neuritis-most common serious s/e), and is contraindicated in children below 6 years.
- **Pyrazinamide** causes hepatitis, hyperuricemia (aspirin can be used), and is slowly acting bactericidal ATT-has cavity sterilizing activity. It should be stopped in case of gout.
- **Streptomycin** is bactericidal ATT with ototoxicity and nephrotoxicty and is most vestibulotoxic aminoglycoside. It is contraindicated in pregnancy due to fear of ototoxicity in developing baby.
- **Cycloserine** is a bacteriostatic drug acting by inhibiting cell wall synthesis. It causes CNS side effects like psychosis, seizures, hallucinations and neuropathies etc. They can be reduced by using B_6.
- Capreomycin, kanamycin and amikacin are used in MDR tuberculosis.

ANTILEPROTIC DRUGS

- **Dapsone** (diamino-disulfone-DDS) is **DOC** for leprosy and dermatitis herpitiformis. It acts by inhibiting folate utilization by bacteria.
- It is a bacteriostatic drug, undergoes enterohepatic circulation and is concentrated in *stratum corneum*. Its most common side effect is haemolysis.
- It also causes megaloblastic aneamia and bone marrow suppression. TEN (toxic epidermal necrolysis) is a rare side effect. Methemoglobinemia and fixed drug eruption also occur.
- Clofazamine (static) is the **longest** acting antileprotic drug ($t_{½}$ = 70 days), has **analgesic** and **anti-inflammatory** actions and causes blue pigmentation of skin.
- **ROM** (Rifampin-600 mg, ofloxacin-200 mg and minocycline-100 mg) regimen is used for single lesions of leprosy.
- **Thalidomide** is DOC for lepra reaction type-2, while glucocorticoids are DOC for type-1.
- **Rifampin** is most active (fastest acting) drug in leprosy. Paucibaciallary leprosy is treated for 6 months while multibacillary for 1 year.

ANTIPARASITIC DRUGS

- **Melarsoprol** is DOC for CNS stage of African trypanosomiasis.
- **Suramin** is DOC for hemolymphatic stage of African trypanosomiasis. It is a long acting drug ($t_{½}$=50 days). CNS toxicity and renal damage can occur.
- **Nifurtimox** is DOC for American trypanosomiasis.
- **Sodium stibogluconate** is DOC for leishmaniasis (both visceral and cutaneous).
- It is one of the pentavalant antimonial and is a first line drug. Half life > 24 hours.
- GI upset and ECG changes can occur. Meglumine is rarely used for same indication.
- **Pentamidine** can cause pancreatitis and diabetes, which may be permanent. It is used in leishmaniasis but is a highly toxic drug.
- Damage to pancreas results into hypoglycemia followed later by hyperglycemia. Hypotension occurs on intravenous injection. The drug is also used in treatment of *pneumocystis carnii.*
- **Miltefostine** is most effective drug against leishmaniasis; others include pentamidine

(causes pancreatitis and permanent diabetes), allopurinol and amphotericin B.

- **Nitazoxanide** is a prodrug and is used for Giardia and Cryptospordium. It is also active against the metronidazole resistant species.
- **Eflornithine**, a inhibitor of ornithine decarboxylase is also used as an antiparasitic drug. Originally it was developed as an anticancer drug.
- But now a days, the drug is used in African trypanosomiasis (also called sleeping sickness). Gastrointestinal upset and neurotoxicity can occur.

ANTIHELMINTHIC DRUGS

- **Albendazole** is DOC for all nematodes helminthic infections except Strongyloides stercoralis (ivermectin is DOC), *W. bancrofti* (dietheyl-carbamazepine is DOC) and Oncocerchiasis (ivermectin is DOC).
- **Lvermectin** is a GABA potentiating drug. Mazzotti's reaction is a rare problem that can occur when ivermectin is used in *onchoserchiasis*. This is due to sudden bursting of larve inside eye.
- **Albendazole** is the DOC for neurocysticercosis. Though, praziquantel can also be used but is NOT the DOC. Drugs should NOT be used in ocular and spinal neurocysticercosis as this can lead to paralytic symptoms.
- Alopecia and raised liver enzymes can occur. Penetration of albendazole increased when it is used along with corticosteroids as opposed to prazequental when the penetration decreases.
- **Mebendazole** is DOC for mass deworming or mixed infestations. Mechanism of action of both albendazole and mebendazole is by paralysing microtubule dependent glucose uptake.

- **Pyrental** stimulates nicotinic receptors while piperazine stimulates GABA receptors. The former causes spastic paralysis while the latter causes flaccid paralysis. Both of them can cause live expulsion of worms and are safe in pregnancy. Pyrental is used in *tricostrongyloids ascaris* and pinworm infections (TAP).
- **Thiabendazole** is most toxic anti-helminthic drug and has analgesic and anti-inflammatory actions. It is past DOC for *cutaneous larva migrans*. Currently, it is treated by albendazole.
- **Niclosamide** is the DOC for intestinal cysticercosis; however, its use should be followed by purgative.
- **Prazequental** is the DOC for all schistosomes (biothionol is an alternative). It acts by modulating calcium entry into parasite and causes contraction of parasite due to hypocalcemic tentany. It can lead to live worm expulsion. Dose of prazequental in neurocysticercosis is **50 mg/kg** for 14 days. Albendazole dose is 15 mg/kg for same duration. **Levamesol** is an anti-worm drug that has immunomodulatory properties that can also lead to live worm expulsion.

Unit 8

Gastrointestinal Drugs

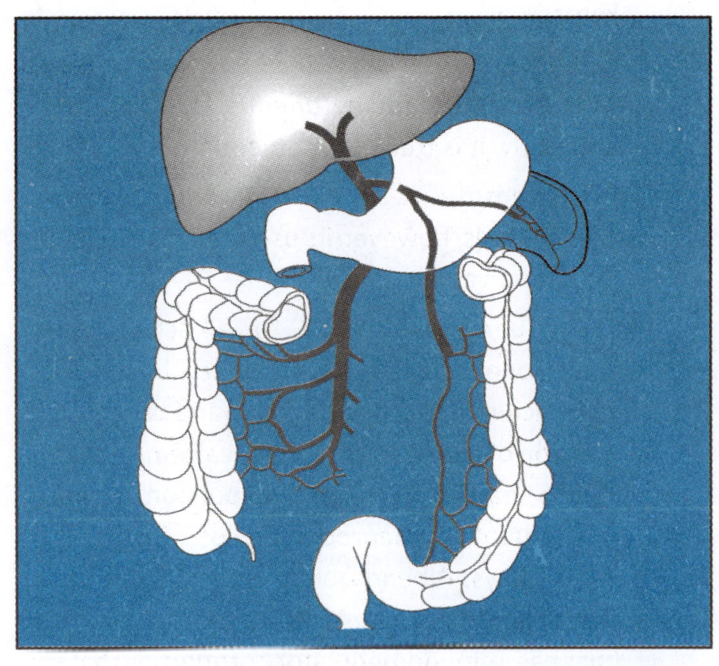

Movement, air and fluids are major worries for GIT

EMETICS, ANTIEMETICS AND PROKINETICS

- **Apomorphine** is used to induce vomiting in poisoning and is given via parenteral route, while *ipecacuhana* is given via oral route.
- Induction of vomiting is contraindicated in kerosene poisoning, acid and alkali poisoning- due to fear of aspiration and perforation.
- **Metoclopramide** is most commonly used antiemetics but is D2 blocker; therefore causes hyperprolactinemia, and extrapyramidal side effects. It is the DOC for shortening gastric emptying time and prevention of aspiration pneumonitis. Extra-pyramidal side effects are common in children and it can also cause hyperprolactinaemia.
- **Domperidone** blocks D2 receptors only in CTZ center and not in basal ganglia, therefore does not cause extra-pyramidal side effects (can even be used in Parkinson patients).
- **Cisapride** is a D4 agonist and is a promotility (prokinetic or motility enhancing) drug with no anti-emetic activity.
- **Cisapride** given with enzyme inhibitors such as erythromycin, azoles, ciprofloxacin can cause

torsade de pointes. Therefore, it is a banned drug in many countries.

- **Mosapride**, itopride etc. are free from *torsade de pointes* causing effect. This is because they do not interact with potassium channels in heart.

Antiulcer Medications

- **Cimetidine** is the oldest and most toxic H2 blocker (causes gynecomastia and taste disturbances-dysgusia-ACE I also cause it). **Ranitidine is free** from gynaecomastia because, it does not interfere with cytochromal enzyme or androgen metabolism.
- **Antacids** are fast acting anti-ulcer drugs but relapse rate is high-aluminum containing antacids cause constipation and intestinal obstruction.
- These reduce the absorption of chloroquine, tetracyclines, itraconazole, iron and fluoroquinolones.
- Sodium bicarbonate is a systemic antacid and gastric distension is the most common side effect of this drug.
- **Aluminum phosphate** is used as a phosphate binder in CRF; it can relax smooth muscles of GIT

and hence can aggravate intestinal obstruction. It is used as a phosphate binder in CRF.

- Magnesium oxide (milk of magnesia) cause diarrhea is also used as laxative.

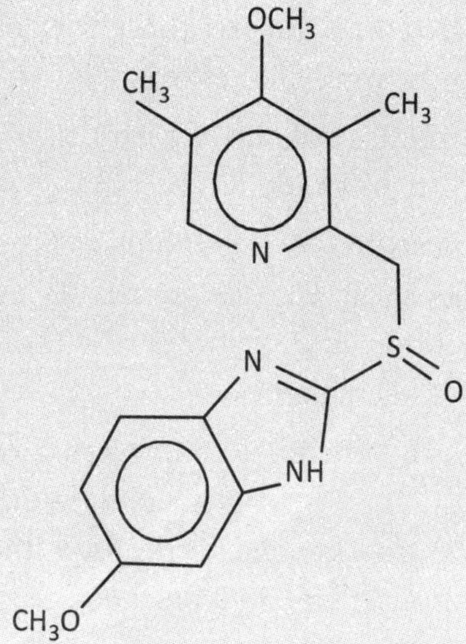

Figure: *Omeprazole*

- **Omeprazole, rabeprazole, esomeprazole, pentaprazole and lansaprazole** etc. drugs are PPIs and are DOCs for all acid related conditions (e.g., peptic ulcers, dyspepsia, reflux esophagitis, Zollinger Ellison's syndrome).
- They are safe drugs and their most common side effect is **abdominal pain.** Hypergastrenemia

occurs in many patients. These block the enzyme Na^+K^+ ATPase irreversibly, therefore act for a longer duration of action.

- **Pirenzipine** and **telanzipine** are selective M1 receptor blockers used in peptic ulcer. They are not popular due to their low efficacy and antimuscarinic side effects.
- They reduce volume of gastric acid. Pirenzepine is a tertiary amine.
- **Misoprostol (PGE1)** is an ulcer protective drug; previously, it was DOC for NSAID induced ulcers prevention now PPIs are DOCs. Its most common side effect is diarrhoea.
- **Bismuth subcitrate, deglycerinihzed liquorice** (has mineralocorticoid effect-aldosterone like effect) are ulcer healing drugs; bismuth has anti-*H. pylori* activity but can cause encephalopathy and osteodystrophy
- **Metronidazole, clarithromycin/ampicillin/PPI** are combination therapy **(triple therapy)** for eradication of *H. pylori.*

DRUGS FOR DIARRHOEA AND CONSTIPATION

- **Loperamide** (a synthetic opioid-LOMOTIL) is the DOC for functional diarrhoea (non-infectious, e.g. travelers diarrhoea)-it is free from disadvantages of opioids e.g. respiratory depression, as it doesn't enter BBB.
- **Diphenoxylate** (Lomofen) is combination of atropine+loperamide and is used as an alternative drug. Diphenoxylate is an opioid, therefore, shares the same disadvantages typical of an opioid.
- **Rifaximin** is a newer drug used for traveler's diarrhoea.
- **Racecadrotil** is a enkephalinase inhibitor and is also used in functional diarrhoeas.
- **Physillium**, bran are bulk laxatives-form bulk induce laxative effect. They are slowest acting laxative.
- **Lactulose** is osmotic laxative and is used in hepatic encephalopathy for bowel cleaning. It is the fastest acting laxative agent.
- **PEG** (polyethylene glycol) solution is used to clean bowel for colonoscopies. It is given in large

amount, hence not well tolerated. Drug acts via osmotic mechanisms.

- **Colistipol/cholestyramine** are used for bile acid induced diarrhea as they bind to bile acids in small gut and avoid irritation of large gut.
- **DOSSS (dioctyl sodium sulpho succinate)** is detergent like drug for used for softening stool or earwax.
- Phenolphthalein, castor oil and bisacodyl are irritant laxatives. Phenolphthalein can cause melanosis coli.
- **Cotrixmoxazole/fluoroquinolones** are antibiotics used in shigella dysentery; otherwise antibiotics are avoided in diarrhoeas.

Unit 9

Respiratory Drugs

Breath for life

- Dry cough is suppressed with drugs like codeine/ dextromethorphan etc. (DOC), while wet cough is encouraged (with expectorant)
- **Bromhexine** is most common mucolytic-rhinorrhoea/lacrymation is its most common side effect. It is used to liquefy the thick and viscid sputum in COPD or cystic fibrosis.
- DOC of initial treatment in bronchial asthma is inhaled beta-2 agonist. These provide quick symptomatic relief.
- Beta-2 agonists act by increasing the level of cAMP with in the cells. Tremor is their most common side effect. Others include hypotension and hyperglycemia.
- **Corticosteroids** are used for persistent asthma and in case of severe persistent they are used orally.
- Theophylline is a **methylxanthine** (inhibits PDE); increases cAMP in smooth muscles–it is a bronchodilator used for poorly controlled asthma and apnoea in premature newborns.
- Most common side effect of theophylline is tremor-more common with ciprofloxacin or erythromycin-combination, seizures and hyper-reflexia occur in high doses.

Dose should be increased in smokers while reduction is needed in neonates, elderly, cardio-pulmonary disorders or those with pneumonia. It follows zero order kinetics.

- **Isoproterenol** is the fastest acting broncho-dilator; acts upon beta-1 and beta-2 receptors. Side effect is cardio-stimulation.
- **Salbutamol** and **terbutaline** are selective beta-2 agonists. These are longer acting and apart from asthma are also useful in hyperkalemia and suppression of unwanted labour.
- **Salmeterol** (duration 12 hours) is slowest acting bronchodilator and hence is contraindicated in acute asthma.
- Bambuterol is longest acting bronchodilator (duration 24 hours).
- **Chromyglycate** sodium is a **mast cell stabilizer** (Not absorbed orally) and is DOC for prevention of exercise-induced asthma, asthma prophylaxis and food allergy. It is given via inhalation route.
- **Zileuton, zafirlekast, montelukast** (not used in acute asthma) are used for aspirin induced asthma. Rare side effect is *Chrug-Struass* syndrome. Monteleukast is more potent than zafirleukast. These are used mainly as oral agents

in asthma as "add on" treatments. These are safe in children.

- **Ipratropium bromide** is DOC for COPD; **anticholinergic** drug causes dry mouth-fungal infections can occur-topical nystatin is used.
- **Ketotifen** is **serotonin** antagonist used for asthma prevention (dose=1 mg/day).

Unit 10

Coagulants and Anticoagulants

Both thinning and thickening of blood produce problems.

COAGULANTS

- **Vitamin K** is a coagulant, DOC for warfarin overdose and aspirin poisoning (used with fresh frozen plasma. It acts by increasing synthesis of factor II, VII, IX, X.
- Most common side effect of vitamin K is flushing. K_1 is most commonly used formulation. Menadiones are contraindicated in newborn due to hemolytic jaundice. It is antidote of warfarin and is also used in aspirin poisoning.

ANTICOAGULANTS

- Warfarin is most commonly used oral anticoagulant, acts by inhibiting synthesis of factor II, VII, IX, X.
- Most common side effect is **bleeding** but also it causes fat and breast necrosis It can occur in patients with protein C or protein S deficiency with equal frequency. Vitamin K is an antidote.
- Anticoagulants (both heparin and warfarin) cause osteopenia and osteoporosis because they inhibit carboxylation of protein **osteonectin**.
- Heparins (hepa: Greek-from liver-discovered by McLean) are of three types physiological (e.g., danapranoid), low molecular weight (Mol. wt. <5000), e.g. enoxaparin) and high molecular weight (molecular weight > 10,000).
- Heparin is **contraindicated** in patients with bleeding peptic ulcers, infective endocarditis, bleeding disorders, intracranial hemorrhage, neurosurgical cases, ocular surgery.
- Do not do lumber puncture in heparinized patients.
- Most common side effect of heparins is bleeding; most common initial manifestation is hematuria.

- Heparin damages the platelets therefore the injured platelets clot together leading to formation of clot (white clot-as it is formed only by platelets).
- Thrombolytic drugs can be used for heparin-induced clotting.
- Enoxaparin, *foundoxaparin* are newer heparins with less risk of bleeding complications.
- **Direct thrombin inhibitors** are anticoagulants that interfere with enzymatic function of thrombin. These are of two types: Univalent and bilavalent. Examples of former include ximelbatran, argatroban and melagatran and lepirudin, bivalrudin, hirudin and desirudin are examples of the latter category. Ximelbatran is banned in many countries as the drug produces hepatic failure.
- **Low molecular weight heparins** are better because of better pharmacokinetics, once a day daily dosing, less chance of bleeding or clotting leading to embolism.
- DOC for heparin overdose is **protamine sulphate**, which is a basic LMWH heparin by itself (1 mg-100 IU of heparin).

THROMBOLYTIC AND FIBRINOLYTIC INHIBITORS

- **Fibrinolytic inhibitors** (also called as anti-plasmin drugs) such as tranhexaenemic acid, epsilon aminocaproic acid, and Aprotinin are used in massive bleeding.
- They are DOC for thrombolytic drugs-induced bleeding (usually intra-cranial).
- Thrombolytic drugs such **streptokinase** (DOC for AMI) act by converting plasminogen to plasmin, which inturn degrades clots.
- Most common side effect of streptokinase is hypotension-antibodies can reduce its effectiveness. Therefore, should not be repeated in the same patient with in a short span of time. Loading dose is 300,000 given as loading dose IV followed by a maintains dose of 50,000 IU.
- **Urokinase and t-PA** are direct plasminogen activators (do not evoke antibodies), anistreplase is longest acting (1-2 hours), streptokinase (20 min) and alteplase, retiplase (<10 min).
- Bleeding is most common side effect-intracranial hemorrhage is most serious complication-they are contraindicated inactive bleed (e.g., ulcer).

- **Antiplasmin drugs** (Aprotinin, epsilon aminoicapronic acid and tranexamic acid) can be given intravenously for the treatment of thrombolytic drug induced bleeding. Their side effect is vascular thrombosis.

Unit 11

Endocrinal Drugs

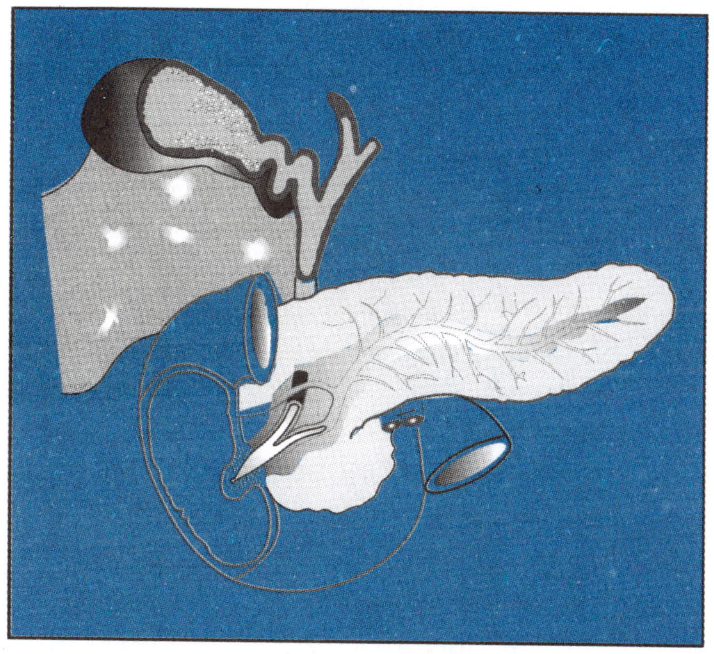

I know nothing except the fact of my ignorance.

—Socrates

PITUITARY HORMONES

- **GnRH analogues** (naferlin, goserlin, buserlin) are DOCs to suppress gonadotrohin secretions in precocious puberty, prostatic cancer, endometriosis, and fibroid uterus.
- **Bromocriptine** (partial agonist of D_1 receptors) is DOC for suppression of unwanted lactation, hyperprolactinemia, acromegaly (carbergoline in pregnancy). Nausea is the most common side effect of bromocriptine.
- Hypotension and psychiatric side effects can occur. it important to know that dopamine agonists of older types are short acting drugs and are poorly tolerated. Therefore, newer agonists (e.g., ropinirole and pramipixole) have been introduced.
- **Somatrem/somatropin** are growth hormone analogues used in short stature patients, e.g., Turner's syndrome (XO).
- **Cosyntropin (ACTH analogue)** is DOC for infantile spasm.
- **Menotropins** (FHS and LH) are used in hypogonadal states.
- **Oxytocin** is used to induce or augment labour; contraindicated renal failure, or hypertension with IHD.
- **Desmopressin (V2 agonist)** is DOC for craniogenic diabetes insipidus; also useful in hemophilia and Von Willebrand's disease.

ADRENAL HORMONES

- **Hydrocortisone** (DOC for congenital adrenal hyperplasia, acute and chronic adrenal insufficiency) is most common glucocorticoid secreted endogenously (10 mg/day).
- Aldosterone is most potent mineralocorticoid (even up to 30 times more potent than fludrocortisone).
- It has equal salt retaining and anti-inflammatory activities. Methylprednisolone, triamcinolone and fluprednisolone have no salt retaining activity.
- **Hydrocortisone** is shortest and least potent glucocorticoid with maximum mineralocorticoid activity. Any patient that has taken a glucocorticoid for more than 2 weeks can have features of glucocorticoid excess. Na^+ retention and K^+ loss is a prominent side effect.
- 76% of glucocorticoids is bound to corticosteroid binding globulin. Its synthesis is increased by pregnancy, estrogens, hypo and hyperthyroidism and protein deficiency.
- **Dexamethasone** has maximum topical activity while hydrocortisone has no topical activity.
- **Dexamethasone/betamethasone** are most potent, longest acting glucocorticoids (act for >24-36 hours); have no salt retaining activity but have maximum anti-inflammatory activity.
- **Desoxycorticosterone acetate** (DOCA) has no glucocorticoids and is pure mineralocticoid.

SEX HORMONES (ESTROGENS, PROGESTERONE)

- FSH, LH, hCG (synthesis-syncytiotrophoblasts-1 week after pregnancy) and inhibition are **glycoprotein** hormones.
- **Estrogen,** LH, and FHS peak at the time of ovulation. hCG peaks 6 weeks after pregnancy. It maintains leuteal function and inhibiting LH release.
- Combinational preparations contain **estrogens** (e.g., ethinyl estradiol and mestranol) and **progesterone** (Norethindrone, norgestrel, ethmoidal diacetate) and are most commonly used type of pills. Estrogens (dose –25-50 microgram) are given for 3 weeks and progesterone is given in last week.
- **Desogesterel, drospirinone and gastodene** are free from androgenic side effects.
- OCPs are of four types: **sequential, biphasic, triphasic** and **morning after pills** (post-coital contraceptives).
- Sequential preparations have been withdrawn due to risk of **endometrial cancer.** It is due to high estrogen content.

Table: Contraindication of OCPs

- A – Adenoma liver
- B – Breast cancer, breast-feeding
- C – Cholestatic jaundice, cirrhosis
- D – Diabetes

- Main **advantages** of OCPs include less risk of anemia, rheumatoid arthritis, and pelvic inflammatory disease. Risk of cancer cervix is unaffected while that of **endometrial** and **ovarian cancer** is reduced. Breast cancer is marginally increased.
- Main **disadvantages** are nausea, vomiting, mystaligia, weight gain, chlosma, benign tumors of liver, thromboembolism and migraine. They should be avoided in women over 35, hypertension, cancer breast, diabetes and recent AMI.
- **Biphasic** and **triphasic** have fixed amount of estrogens but varied amount of progesterone. This is to reflect changes in menstrual cycle. This prevents irregular or breakthrough bleed.
- **Minipills** are progesterone-containing pills and have got lower efficacy (high failure rate). These act not by inhibiting ovulation but by making cervical mucous thick.
- These are suitable for lactating and women over 35 years of age. They do not affect the quality and quantity of milk.

- **Diethylstilbestrol** (DES) is given 50 mg for 5 days and should be continued despite nausea for post-coital contraception.
- Two **Overall tablets**, 12 hours apart can also be used. Levonorgestrel (i pill) is also getting increasingly popular as a postcoital contraceptive.
- **Medroxyprogesterone acetate** (Depo-Provera) is given one injection every 3 months. Major advantage is compliance and safety. It does not cause embolic events. Gall bladder disease and osteoporosis can however occur.
- **Thromboembolism** occurs due to estrogen component and is dose dependent.
- **Levonorgestrel** (Norplant) is progesterone suited for long-term contraception (3-5 years). It releases 30-85 ng\ml of the drug; if implanted within 7 days of menstruation, it starts acting from the same day. It slightly Increases the risk of ectopic pregnancy.
- **Selective serotonin estrogen receptor modulators** (SERMs) are agonists–antagonists of estrogen receptors. They are blockers of estrogens on one receptor, while stimulators at others. For example, tamoxifen causes increase in bone density (estrogenic) effect and is DOC for prevention of breast cancer (anti-estrogen effect).

DRUGS FOR INFERTILITY

- **Clomiphene citrate** is DOC for ovulation induction. It is a partial agonist of estrogen receptors; it increases gonadotropins by inhibiting the negative feedback. It does so by blocking the estrogen receptors in hypothalus resulting into increase in LH and FSH release.
- **It increases FSH and LH** in men, which increases gametogenesis and steroidogenesis.
- It's most common side effect is ovarian cysts, enlargement and multiple births. It is **ineffective** in postmenopausal women. **It is most common cause of multiple births.**
- There are two main gonadotrophins human menopausal gonadtrophin (FSH, LH) MENOTROPIN (FSH).
- These stimulate ovarian follicles but require hCG to induce ovulation. Multiple birth and ovarian hyper-stimulation syndrome can occur.
- GnRh analogues include nafarelin, goeserline and buserlin. Mode of administration determines their therapeutic effect. Given in a pulsatile manner the release is enhanced while given continuously, the release is reduced.
- These are useful in hypogonadism and anovulatory infertility when given in pulsatile

manner. Given continuously, they are used in endometriosis and cancer prostate.

Table: Contraindication of Gonadotropins

- Pituitary tumor
- Ovarian failure
- Ovarian cyst, tumor, or enlargement
- Raised intracranial pressure
- Pregnancy
- Bleeding

- **RU 486** (Russel Uclaff-486), also called as mifepristone is progesterone antagonist with antiglucocorticoid activities. It is the DOC for first trimester abortion along with misoprostol. By inhibiting progesterone support to uterus, it causes leuteolysis. It is also used in meningioma, fibroid uterus and Cushing's disease.

MALE SEX HORMONES

- **Testosterone** is the main male sex hormone synthesized in testis, ovary and adrenal cortex.
- **Stanazolol, methypyralone, fluoxymesterone and nandrolone** are anabolic steroids. These are used to increase muscle mass illicitly by athletes.
- Therapeutically, they are sometimes used in bedridden patients and those with HIV related muscle wasting. Their use can cause **cholestatic hepatitis,** and **gynaecomastia.** Testicular atrophy can also occur.
- FSH in males is needed for spermatogenesis due to its actions on seminiferous tubules.
- LH increases testosterone synthesis by **Leydig cells.** 17-alpha-alkylated derivates of testosterone are orally active and examples include; methyltestosterone, fluoxymesterone, oxandrolone and norethindrone. Jaundice and liver damage is common with them.
- Side effects of **androgens** include; male pattern baldness, menstrual irregularities, premature closure of epiphyseal cartilage and masculinization of female baby once exposed in utero.
- Inhibition of gonadotrophin release can cause testicular atrophy and gynaecomastia.

Antiandrogens

- **Gossypol** is a phenolic derivative of cotton plant; it is known as male contraceptive.
- **Hypokalemia** and muscle weakness are its common side effects.
- **Flutamide, biclutamide** and **cyproterone** acetate are the antagonists of testosterone.

Table: Uses of anti-androgens

- Precocious puberty
- Cancer of prostate
- Male pattern baldness
- Virilizing syndromes
- Inhibiting excessive sex derive in men and women

- **Finasteride** is inhibitor of 5-alpha reductase and acts by blocking the conversion of testosterone to dihydrotestosterone.
- It is useful in patients with large prostates and those with cancer of prostate and male pattern baldness.
- Dutasteride is a dual drug and blocks both isoforms of the enzyme 5-alpha reductase (I and II).

THYROID HORMONES

- **Thyroxine T4** is most abundant thyroid hormone. 99% of T4 protein bound. And controls the rate of metabolic processes in the body and influencing physical development.
- **Thyroxine** (less active), T3 (more active) are DOCs for myoxedema, cretinism (usual dose is 25 microgram/day). T4 is longer acting and is more protein bound.
- **Thionamides** (propylthiouracil, carbamezole, methimazole etc. are antithyroid drugs acting by inhibiting thyroid hormone synthesis (inhibit thyroid peroxides).
- **Propylthiouracil** is highly protein bound anti-thyroid drug (DOC for hyperthyroidism in pregnancy and thyroid storm).
- **Methimazole** is the most potent and longest acting anti-thyroid drug, while propylthiouracil is shortest acting.
- Most common serious side effect of anti-thyroid drugs is **agranulocytosis** (indicated by sore throat or fever-withdraw the drug). It is immune mediated. Count of neutrophils are not helpful in predicting outcome. But we should stop when counts fall below 500 cells/cmm^3. Hepatitis and

vasculitis are other side effects. Aplasia cutis is a rare side effect of methimazole given in pregnancy.

- **Lugol's iodine** acts by inhibiting release of thyroid hormones (DOC for making gland firm before surgery)
- **Radioactive iodine** (I^{131} acts by delivering *beta* and *gamma* rays); destroys thyroid gland and is contraindicated in young patients due to fear of carcinogenesis.
- Papillary cancer of thyroid gland is most common cancer induced by this drug. It is treated by T4 oral supplementation as it is dependent upon TSH stimulation.
- Propranolol is DOC of **initial choice** for toxic multi-nodular goiter. It can also be used for prevention of thyroid storm.

ANTIDIABETIC DRUGS

- 100 million people have diabetes worldwide and 10% of Indians are diabetics.
- **Insulin** is a polypeptide with mol. weight (5000) acting by tyrosine kinase receptors (auto-phosphorylation receptors)-Benting and Best discovered it.
- It is a hypoglycemic hormone, while glucagon, GH, cortisol and adrenaline are counter regulatory hormones increasing blood sugar.
- It is synthesized as a preprohormone. Neither preproinsulin nor proinsulin or C peptide have any hypoglycemic action.
- Zinc is added exogenously to increase shelf-life of insulin. In the body, it is present as a hexamer.
- Insulin inhibits phosphoenolcarboxykinase, (PEP-CK) phosphorylase (musle and liver); stimulates hexokinase and lipoprotein lipase (LPL).
- Insulin is a short acting hormone with half-life is 2-5 minutes. Exogenously administered insulin is metabolized in kidneys, while endogenously produced insulin is metabolized mainly in liver by insulin reductase.
- Most common side effect is hypoglycemia, beta-blockers can potentate silent hypoglycemia as they block somatic manifestations.

- **Human insulin** causes lipodystrophy; zinc is added to insulin to increase shelf-life and stability of solution
- **Insulin lispro** is shortest acting, while insulin glargine is longest acting.
- **Sulphonylureas** increase insulin release, increase number of insulin receptors and insulin sensitivity.
- Tolbutamide is **safest** sulphonylureas; while chlorpropamide is worse (hypoglycemia is most likely, causes SIADH, disulfiram like reaction).
- **Glimepride** is most potent and longest acting sulphonylureas of newer generation. Its mechanism of action is unique so even may work in patients resistant to other sulphonylureas. Less likely to cause hypoglycemia, therefore can even be combined with insulin.
- **Chlorpropamide** is most toxic, longest acting sulphonyluireas and is most likely to cause hypoglyecemia. It also causes SIADH and disulfiram like reaction. It should be avoided in elderly patients.
- Hypoglycemia is the most common of the sulfonylureas. It is more common with drugs that are metabolized to an active metabolite with significant renal excretion.

- These agents include chlorpropamide and glyburide, both of which should be avoided in the setting of impaired renal function and used with caution in elderly patients. Glipizide and glimepiride are associated with a lower incidence of hypoglycemia.
- **Bigunides** (Metformin and phenformin) act by inhibiting hepatic output of glucose (inhibit glycogenolysis). Phenformin is banned due to lactic acidosis.
- **Metformin** causes less lactic acidosis, doesn't cause hypoglycemia, and is DOC for obese diabetic patients (most common-s/e-dyspepsia); poorly tolerated due to adverse GI side effects.
- It is also used in polycystic ovarian disease and prevention of type-2 diabetes. It is contraindicated in COPD, CHF, severe renal or hepaic failure. It is only oral hypopglycemic that doesn't cause weight gain. It may decrease B_{12} absorption and cause megaloblastic anaemia.
- **Acarbose** is alpha-glucosidase inhibitor, can even be used in IDDM-MC side effect is dyspepsia. It is contraindicated in severe liver disease and intestinal obstruction and IBD.
- **Thiozolidinediones** (trogliatazone, piogliatazone) are insulin sensitizers. They modulate peroxisome

proliferator receptor activated protein-gamma (PRAP-gamma) expression and increase receptor sensitivity. Edema and weight gain is a common side effect.

- **Magletinide** derivatives act in same manner as insulin (secretagogues). Main advantage is that they release insulin only at time of meals.
- GMT (glucosidase inhibitors, metformin and thiozolidinediones) have antihyperglycemic activity.
- **Exenatide** (GLP-1 analogue-glucagon like peptide) and **pramlintide** (Amyelin analogue) are the newer antidiabetic drugs that are given parenterally like insulin. These drugs have unique mechanism of actions.

DRUGS ACTING ON CALCIUM METABOLISM

- **Calcium** is most abundant mineral in the body. 1 kg of calcium (99% in bone) and half kg of phosphate is found in body.

Classification of drugs acting on calcium metabolism:

Nutrient

Calcium

Vitamin D

Hormones

PTH

Calcitonin

Biphosphonates

Alendronate

Pamindroate

Risendronate

Etidronate

Ibandronate

- **Parathormone** (84 amino acid) is has dual mechanism of calcium. In low dosages, it increases the bone strength, while in high dosages, it causes bone resorption. Its major physiological effect is to maintain calcium levels.

It does so by increasing calcium absorption from gut.

- **Teriparatide** is a synthetic PTH analogue used for prevention of postmenopausal osteoporosis. Teripartide is a newer analogue of PTH that is also used for osteoporosis.
- Albumin is the most common calcium binding protein carrying 40% of total calcium. Remaining is bound to phosphate and citrate and includes free calcium.
- PTH, vitamin D and calcitonin are major factors regulating calcium and phosphate levels.
- **Calcitonin** is 34 amino acid hormone that lowers calcium levels by increasing cellular uptake, increasing excretion and by increasing bone formation.
- It is the DOC (salmon calcitonin) for bone pain due to cancers and **Paget's disease.**
- **Bisphosphonates** are used to prevent and treat osteoporosis. They act by inhibiting bone resorption by osteoclasts.

  Importantly, estrogens also work by similar mechanism. These increase bone density and prevent fractures.

- **Alendronate** can cause reflux esophagitis. Therefore, the patient should not lie down for half an hour following drug intake.
- **Bisphosphonates** are not metabolized in the body. Hence, these are avoided in renal failure.

Unit 12

Anticancer and Immunosuppressive Drugs

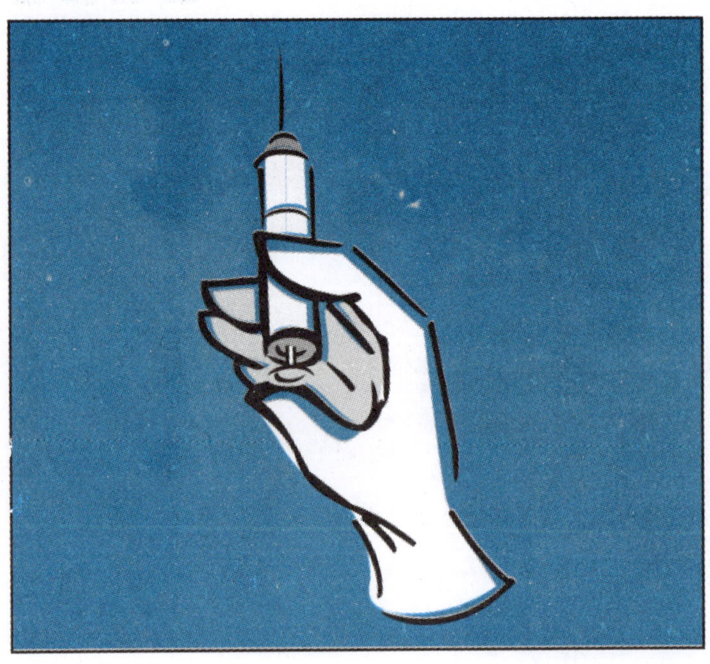

Some drugs cure or kill.
—Unknown

- **Alkylating agents** form covalent bonds, are radiomimetic agents; they kill the tumor cells by apoptosis and necrosis.
- **Mechlorethamine (used in MOPP regimen)** is the oldest anticancer drug, it is vesicant. Therefore, gloves should be worn before its administration.
- **Nitrosoureas** are the DOCs for brain cancers; these cause delayed bone marrow depression and pulmonary fibrosis.
- Chlorambucil is the past DOC for CLL, currently, the DOC is fludarabine.
- **Bone marrow depression** is the most common toxicity of alkylating agents.
- **Melphalan** is the DOC for multiple myeloma; it has least nausea causing potential.
- **Platinum compounds** (Cisplatin, Carboplatin and Oxaliplatin) have maximum emetogenic, ototoxic and nephrotoxic potential. These are used in cervical cancers.
- **Doxorubicin** is broadest spectrum anticancer drug, it causes free radical mediated cardiotoxicity (Dexrozoxane is DOC). Antitumor antibiotics act by inhibiting DNA function. It can activate *topo-isomerase-1.*

- **Dactinomycin** (actinomycin D-DOC for Wilms tumor), plicamycin (also called mithramycin) are other antibiotics inhibiting DNA directed RNA synthesis and affect rapidly dividing and stationary cells equally.
- It is the drug of 2nd choice for ectopic pregnancy after methotrexate.
- **Cyclophosphamide** causes hemorrhagic cystitis (MESNA is DOC). It is used in Hodgkin, CML, cancer ovary and cancer breast (DOC) and is not used in endometerial carcinoma.
- Cystitis can be prevented by adequate hydration.
- Acrolein is the major metabolite responsible for causing hemorrhagic necrosis.
- **5-fluorouracil** is a pyrimidine analogue with no phase specificity. It is the drug of choice for colorectal cancer, also used for liver cancer with secondaries and cancer of stomach and liver.

  Its most common side effect is GI upset followed by bone marrow suppression. Its rare side effect includes **"hand foot disease".** Since it inhibits the enzyme, thymidylate synthetase, it can produce "thymineless death".
- **Topical 5-FU** is applied to basal cell carcinoma (TOC-radiotherapy) and mycosis fungoids.

Flucytosine is an anticancer drug and gets converted into 5-FU inside the body.

- **Irinotecan** is used in 5-FU resistant tumors while cituximab (EGF inhibitor) is used in metastatic variety of colorectal tumors refractory to irinotecan. Irinotecan can produce diarrhoea as the drug is anticholinesterase. **Oxaliplatin** is another alternative.
- **Busulphan** is specific for granulocytes though other cell lines are also affected. It is most myelotoxic drug. It is the past drug of choice for CML.
- Presently, the DOC is **imatinib mesylate**. It is a tyrosine kinase inhibitor and blocks the interaction resulting from bcl-abr translocation (9 to 22 translocation).
- It has also been approved in the year 2003 for gastrointestinal stromal tumors. Its side effects are non-specific like nausea, edema and abdominal pain etc. Hyperuricemia and skin pigmentation can occur due to busulphan.
- All anti-metabolites except 5-FU have **phase selectivity.**
- **Methotrexate** is antifolate drug inhibiting DHFR other inhibitors are:

C-chloroguanide

P-pyrimethamine

M-methotrexate

T-trimethoprim.

- It is the DOC for ectopic pregnancy, pustular psoriasis and choriocarcinoma (use cyclophosphamide or actinomycin-D in resistant cases).
- Most common side effect is **hepatic fibrosis. Leukovorin rescue** can reduce toxicity but folic acid is not useful. This is because; it does not penetrate into cells. Intrathecal injection can cause 'leukoencephalopathy'.
- **Bleomycin** (most common side effect is pulmonary fibrosis-it is dose-limiting) causes minimal bone marrow suppression. It is a complex glycopeptide.
- **Vinca-alkaloids** (vincristine and vinblastine-cause bone marrow suppression) cause peripheral neuropathy.
- All of these drugs are M-Phase specific. Paraesthesia are initial manifestations. Deep tendon reflexes are lost later.
- **Cyclosporine** is most common immunosuppressive drug, acts by binding to cyclophillins and reduce expression of IL-2 in T-lymphocytes.

- Tacrolimus works by similar mechanism and both of them are known as calcineurine inhibitors. Most common side effect is hypertension and beta-blockers and calcium channel blockers treat it.
- It also causes **hepatitis** and **nephrotoxicity.** Importantly, it does not cause bone marrow suppression. Bleomycin, streptozotocin are other drugs not causing bone marrow suppression
- **Azathioprine**, given with allopurinol should be used in reduced doses to avoid bone marrow toxicity. 6-thioguanine is not a substrate for xanthine oxidase and hence safe with allopurinol. **Allopurinol** is the DOC for tumor-induced hyperuricemia.
- **L-asparaginase** causes pancreatitis and hypersensitivity reactions. It is commonly used to induce remission in childhood leukemias.
- **Etoposide** is a topoisomerase-2 inhibitor while camptothecans like irinotecans (e.g., topotecan/ irinotecan) are inhibitors of topoisomerase I. Irinotecan also has anticholinesterase activity.
- **Amifostine** is DOC for reducing anti-cancer drug associated toxicity. It is a SH donating drug.

Unit 13

Psycho-pharmacology

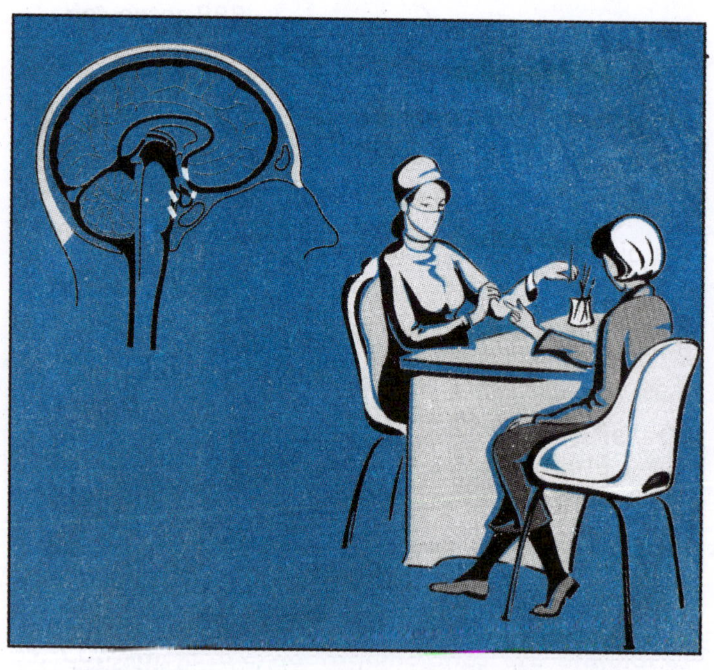

There are no problems apart from the mind

—Krisnamurti

ANTIMANICS (MOOD STABILERS)

- **Lithium** is a monovalent ion and is DOC for acute mania. It is not metabolized and has half-life 20 hours ($Time_{PSSC} = t_{½} \times 5$ i.e. 20 × 5 =100 hours).
- It would take about 4-5 days to achieve plasma steady state concentration. It was discovered by J. Cade in 1949 and acts by *inhibiting* PIP2 recycling.
- It was discovered by James Cade, an Australian psychiatrist.
- **Prophylactic concentration** of lithium is 0.6-0.8 meq/liter and **therapeutic** concentration is 0.8-1.2 meq/liter.

  Values beyond 1.5 ng/ml are toxic. Beyond 2.5 meq/liter, hemodialsis is needed.
- Its most common side effect is GI upset, others are tremors, nephrogenic diabetes insipidous, hypo and hyperthyroidism, acne like eruption, slurring of speech.
- Its most common drug interaction occurs with thiazides which could increase its levels. The drug is eliminated unchanged by kidneys. Therefore, it is avoided in renal failure.
- In rapid cyclers; hypo and hyperthyrodism are more common and **sodium valproate** is the DOC for such patients.

ANTIDEPRESSANTS

- Depression is sadness for two weeks in the presence of pervasive change in mood. It is the most common cause of suicide.
- Antidepressants are well absorbed with large volume of distribution. They have high first pass metabolism.
- **Fluoxetine** is longest acting ($t_{½}$ = 72-96 hours) and most commonly used antidepressant. It is preferred in defaulters with depression due to its long half-life. Drug can delay ejaculation latency.
- **Nefazadone** is the shortest acting antidepressant ($t_{½}$ = 2 hours); it needs to be given several times, hence has lower compliance.
- Paroxetine is SSRI with maximum **anticholinergic** side effects while **doxepine** has maximum such property out of tricyclic antidepressants.
- **Fluoxamine** is enzyme inhibitor, hence causes several drug interactions.
- MAO B is found inside brain. **Tranylcypromine**, a MAO-A inhibitor has stimulant effect on ECG, rest of them have minimal effects. **Moclobamide**

is the safest **MAO A** inhibitor and is reversible in nature. It is not associated with *cheese reaction*.

- However, it should be avoided in patients with epilepsy.
- Consumption of foods with high **tyramine** content (cheese, beer, wine, and meat) can precipitate hypertensive crises.
- **Bupropion** is selective dopamine reuptake inhibitor; and is the DOC for smoking cessation. It should not be given to patients with epilepsy.

ANTIPSYCHOTICS

- Psychosis are severe disturbances of thought and Schizophrenia is most common type of thought disorder (auditory hallucinations of 3rd person type is most characteristic feature).
- Phenothiazines are the oldest antipsychotic drugs. These are D2 backers, alpha-blockers, anti-cholinergic property.

Table: Uses of phenothiazines*

- Schizophrenia
- Schizoaffective disorders
- Borderline personality disorders
- Reduce excitement in acute mania
- Heat stroke
- Hiccups

*Atypical antipsychotics preferred now.

- They are well absorbed, have high first pass metabolism, have weak plasma protein binding, act upon various receptors and have sedative potential.
- **Chlorpromazine** (Largectil-**Laborit** synthesized it) is the most commonly phenothiazines as it is cheap, easily available and has got long safety

record. It is low potency anti-psychotic hence causes sedation and hypotension.

- **Chlorpromazine** is the anti-psychotic drug, but is the DOC for hiccups and hyperthermia. Sedation and hypotension is most common side effects. Piperazine derivatives such as fluphenazine are most potent phenothiazines drugs.
- Cholestatic jaundice and agranulocytosis occur with chlorpromazine. Many patients develop hyperpigmentation.
- Overall, the **most potent** antipsychotic is haloperidol and **least potent** is Thioridazine. Highly potent antipsychotic drugs have extrapyramidal side effects.
- Most common chronic EPS is tardive dyskinesia while in adults; the most common EPS is akathesia and acute muscular dystonia.
- **Promethazine** is the DOC for acute EPS, while propranolol is DOC for akathesia. Diazepam is the DOC for chronic EPS. Importantly, tardive dyskinesia develops due to DA receptor supersensitivity and cholinergic deficiency. Hence, anti-cholinergic drugs are contraindicated as they would worsen it. Tetrabenazine is a new dopamine depletor used in tardive dyskinesia.

- **Thioridazine** is preferred in patients bothered by extrapyramidal side effects (maximum anticholinergic property).
- It can interfere with brown colour vision and can cause **"retitinitis pigmentosa"** type illness. It is **cardiotoxic** drug especially in overdose.
- **Clozapine** is the D4 blocker and is the DOC for patients with EPS, **negative symptoms** and those with treatment resistant schizophrenia.
- It can cause agranulocytosis. It lowers the seizure threshold (2% risk) and should be avoided in patients with epilepsy. Clozapine has been linked with hyperglycemia and hyperlipidemia. The drug also causes myocarditis.
- Newer drugs like **risperidone, sertindole**, and **quetiapine** are free from EPS causing potential; especially at low dose.

  They block 5-HT2A and D4 receptors and are NOT D2 blockers. **Sertindole** and **quitiapine** can cause QT prolongation. **Aripiperazole** and **ziprasidone** are partial agonists of dopamine receptors.
- **Olanzapine** is a clozapine congener, however, that does not cause agranulocytosis. It is anti-cholinergic. Weight gain, diabetes and metabolic syndrome occur as side effects.

- **Haloperidol** is the **DOC** for delirium, chorea, Gille's de La Tourette syndrome. EPS are dose limiting side effects.
- **Penfluridol** is the longest acting antipsychotic drug that is used for remitting and relapsing schizophrenia.
- Loxapine is an **antipsychotic** drug of atypical type that gives rise to amoxapine, which is used in agitated (psychotic) depression.
- Trazadone is DOC for retarded depression due to its stimulant properties. It also achieves penile erection hence is useful in depressed patients with erection. Heavy sedation in a side effect.

Unit 14

Anaesthesia

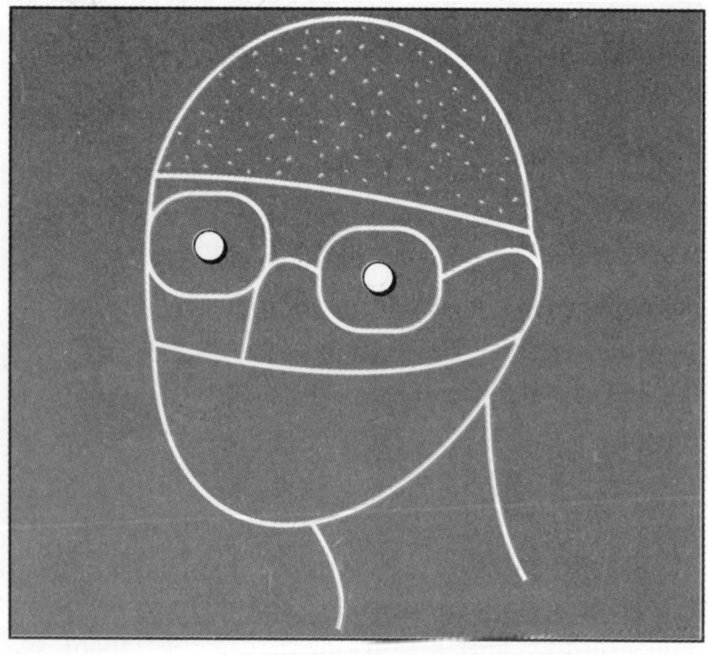

Some must be awake when someone sleeps.
—Unknown

LOCAL ANESTHESIA

- Local anesthetics are drugs producing reversible impairment of neurotransmission in a restricted area of the body.
- They are of two types: esters (bad types-have hypersensitivity and allergic reactions) and **amides** (good types-no hypersensitivity, are longer acting, less toxic).
- Most LAs are weak bases and have water-soluble and lipid soluble parts; have pKa values in physiological pH rage.
- **Cocaine** is the only local anesthetic producing *severe vasoconstriction* (do not give it IV) as it is an indirectly acting *sympathomimetic*.
- It is euphoric and jet-black tongue is characteristic of cocaine abuse.
- **Chloroprocaine** is the shortest LA ($t_{½}$ = <1 min) and is neurotoxic (causes *cauda equina syndrome* if given in spinal canal).
- **Tetracaine** is used as rarely hypobaric anaesthesia. Bupivacaine, mepivacaine and ropivacaine are not used in topical anaesthesia.
- **B** fibers are first to be affected followed by **C** fibers and **A** fibers (Erangeler-Gesser classifica-

tion) (**BCA**-Bachelor of Computer **A**pplication). **C**-fibrers are however first affected followed by B fibers in case of spinal anesthesia (CBA).

- Autonomic Fibers are first to be affected followed by Sensory and Motor (last to be blocked)-**ASM**-Assistant Station Master
- **Sympathetic** fibers are first to be blocked followed by parasympathetic fibers.
- Temperature is the **first** sensation to be blocked followed by touch and pressure. Cold is affected earlier than hot sensation.
- Node of Ranvier is the **first part of nerve** to be blocked followed by rest of the nerve.
- Esters are metabolized in plasma, while amide types are metabolized in liver.
- They are bound to alpha-glycoproteins and hence should be **avoided** in presence of severe liver disease.
- Cocaine is the only LA producing vasoconstriction, it is a drug of abuse and can **increase** the blood pressure. It should therefore be avoided by intravenous route. It can cause tectile hallucinations and presence of **jet-block** tongue is characteristic of cocaine abuse.

- Procaine is the LA of choice in malignant hyperthermia.
- Lidocaine **(amide type)** is most common LA acting for 1 hour (Bupivacaine works for 3 hours). Its dose without adrenaline is 3 mg/kg, while with adrenaline 7 mg/kg. It is avoided in malignant hyperthermia and in patients with a history of or active liver disease.
- Tetracaine is sometimes used as **hypobaric anaesthesia.**
- Bupivacaine is **cardiotoxic**, therefore **should not be** used in **Bier's** block (Lidocaine is DOC)– bupivacaine is used most commonly in obstetrical anesthesia. **Prilocaine** is an alternative drug for this indication.
- Ropivacaine is less likely but levo-bupivacaine is **free** from cardiotoxicty.
- Prilocaine is **safest** LA but causes methaemoglobinemia. It can be used in patients with allergy to lidocaine; in case the patient has allergy to esters and amides both-diphenhydramine can be used.
- Most side effect of spinal anesthesia is **hypotension** (DOC-**ephedrine** - initially, **Trendelenberg's** position is used).

- Crystalloid preloading can prevent the spinal anesthesia induced hypotension.
- **Adrenaline** increases duration (adrenaline increases duration of lidocaine from 1 to 3 hours, Bupivacaine duration increases from 2 to 3 hours). Adrenaline containing lidocaine is contraindicated for ring block of tissues with end arteries **(tip of penis, toe, finger, pinna, nose).**

GENERAL ANAESTHESIA

- Ether was described by Morton; ether is **inflammable**. It is given by open drop method.
- Ether is **best** muscle relaxant GA while trielene is best analgesic GA. Ether should not be given through closed circuit.
- Main **disadvantage of ether** is that it is inflammable while main advantage is its simplicity of administration.
- It is only GA that maintains BP and HR (due to adrenaline release), does not cause adrenaline sensitization of heart and though it is trachio-bronchial irritant but also increases muco-ciliary clearance.
- **Nitrous oxide** (N_2O, laughing gas) is **least potent** GA with highest MAC value (105). It is good analgesic and poor muscle relaxant. It is the DOC for **dental** and **obstetrical analgesia**. It is heavier than air and is 35 times more soluble in blood compared to nitrogen. It causes **2nd gas effect** and **diffusion hypoxia** during recovery. It expands the body cavities; hence it is contraindicated in pneumothorax, acute intestinal obstruction, and middle year surgery. **Megaloblastic anaemia** is a rare side effect.

- Halothane is **least value of MAC** (Most potent-MAC-0.75). It is least irritant GA, and is DOC for external cephalic version and manual removal of placenta.
- It causes hepatitis, which is autoimmune in nature and increase in trichloroacetic acid content of urine indicates imminent hepatitis. It is a poor analgesic and muscle relaxant. Unlike ether it is not inflammable.
- Halothane **sensitizes** heart to action of adrenaline (Cyclopropane also does the same), therefore, halothane causes **arrhythmia**. Adrenaline is **contraindicated** with halothane.
- DOC for neurosurgery is **isoflurane**. It is safe in IHD but causes coronary steal phenomena. It is the DOC for patients in renal failure, hepatic failure, neuro-surgical cases, hypotensive anesthesia, cardio-thoracic and cardiac cases.
- **Enflurane** is contraindicated in epilepsy and produces maximum respiratory depression. **Desflurane** is fastest while **sevoflurane** is without smell (tolerated well even by children).
- Thiopentone is most common inducing agent, antanalgesic, causes thrombosis and gangrene if injected in arteries accidentally. **Needle should**

not be removed, and papaverine/phentolamine should be injected.

- It is an ultra-short acting barbiturate causes loss of consciousness in arm-brain circulation time-11 seconds). Thiopentone is **safe** in malignant hyperthermia.
- **Ketamine (dissociative anesthesia),** is good analgesic, increases ICT, IOP, BP, HR, and is safe in asthma.
- Most common side effect is emergence delirium (DOC-diazepam). It is DOC for painful procedures in children.
- **Etomidate** suppresses adrenal cortex, causes myoclonic movements and has maximum nausea causing potential.
- Propofol is **DOC for day care surgery**, and has **anti-emetic** activity. It also is **anti-pruritic** and causes **injection related pain** (thick 1% egg albumin solution). It is a GABA stimulant.

MUSCLE RELAXANTS

- **Neuromuscular** blockers are of two types: depolarization and non-depolarization blockers.
- Dantrolene sodium, a rynodine receptor blocker is the DOC for malignant hyperthermia.
- Succinylcholine **is most common depolarizing blocker causes twitching, and typical phase-1, phase-2 block (MC s/e-muscle weakness, HYPERKALEMIA).**
- Succinylcholine is contraindicated in burns, tetanus, polio, muscle dystrohies, CVA, trauma, renal failure with hyperkalemia.
- In pseudocholinesterase deficiency, **it causes prolonged apnoea.**
- Mivacurium is **shortest** acting non-depolarizing muscle relaxant, while succinylcholine is the shortest acting depolarizing and overall muscle relaxant.
- Doxacurium **is longest and most potent muscle relaxant.**
- d-Tubocurarine (d-TC) is most potent in histamine release, ganglion blockade and hypotension.
- **Atracurum** is metabolized without enzyme, known as **Hoffmann's elimination** therefore safe

in renal failure, hepatic failure and myesthesia gravis.

- **Fentanyl-droperidol (1:50) combination** is neurolept analgesia, it is also known as INOVAR.
- It can be converted into neurolept anesthesia by use of 50% N_2O and 50% O_2 **(ENTONOX).** It is used for stereotactic brain surgeries.
- Balanced anesthesia means adequate combination of muscle relaxanation, general anaesthesia and inducing agent.
- Baclofen is a $GABA_B$ agonist and is used for atypical facial pain and spasticity of multiple sclerosis. Respiratory depression can occur.

Unit 15

Toxicology

I am not one of those who in expressing opinions confine themselves to facts.

—Mark Twain

- Dimercaprol **(BAL)** has two SH groups, which interact with sulfhydryl containing enzymes in the body-contraindicated in **iron** and **cadmium** poisoning. It is useful in acute poisoning but should not be used in chronic lead poisoning. This is because, it can **redistribute** the lead from periphery to brain. Most common side effect is hypotension.
- EDTA is **polydentate** chelator used in lead intoxication but not in Hg poisoning.
- Its most common side effects are nephrotoxicity and hypocalcemia.
- Succimer is the safest chelator and is used **orally** for lead and mercury poisoning.
- Penicillamine is used for copper, lead, mercury, zinc and is DOC for Wilson's disease; also DOC for cystinuria.
- It can cause pemphigus like eruption, nephrotoxicity and Steven-Johanson syndrome.
- Zinc acetate and trientene are other chelators used in Wilson's disease.
- **Deferroxamine** (1 gm for 85 mg) is obtained from actinomycetes (bacterial product) -iron chelator- most common side effect is hypotension on IV injection. Both EDTA and deferroxamine are

polydentate chelators and rest of them are bidentate.

- **Deferiprone** is a new iron chelator for patients receiving multiple blood transfusions. It is an alternative of deferroxamine.

Unit 16

Phases of Clinical Trials

Innovation is the Key to Success—Unknown

PHASE I CLINICAL TRIAL

In phase I clinical trial candidate drug is tested in healthy volunteers for the first time and is conducted on 20-100 healthy volunteers. The primary parameters tested in Phase I studies are:

- Safety and tolerability
- Pharmacokinetics
- Pharmacodynamics

Qualified persons required for phase I studies are investigator trained in Good Clinical Practices (GCP), healthcare personnel, phlebotomist and site staff. Such studies could be done in patients also specially when the anticancer drugs are being developed.

PHASE II CLINICAL TRIAL

In phase II clinical trials researchers evaluate the efficacy of candidate drug, effectiveness in about 100-500 patients with the disease or condition under study and examine the short- term side effects (adverse events) and risks associated with the drug. They also strive to answer these questions: Is the drug working by expected mechanism? and does it improve the condition in question? Researchers analyze the optimal dose strength and schedules for using the drug. If the drug continues to show promise, researchers prepare for larger phase III clinical trials.

PHASE III CLINICAL TRIAL

In phase III clinical trials researchers study the drug candidate in a larger number (about 1,000 - 5,000) of patients to generate statistically significant data about safety, efficacy, and over all benefit-risk relationship of the drug. This phase of research is key in determining whether the drug is safe and effective. Phase III clinical trials are both costliest and longest. There must be a control group in this phase, and the subjects are randomly allocated to **test** and **control** arm. For this reason phase III is called as **randomized controlled trial (RCT).**

PHASE IV CLINICAL TRIAL

Research on new medicines continues even after approval. As a much larger number of patients begin to use drug, companies must monitor it carefully and submit periodic report including adverse events to regulatory authorities. In addition the regulatory authority sometimes requires a company to conduct additional studies on an approved drug in Phase IV studies. These trials can be set up to evaluate long term safety or how the new medicine affects a specific sub-group of patients. This is called **post-marketing surveillance.**

The adverse events can be reported by the Investigator, registered pharmacist, and healthcare personnel to the CDSCO.

Unit 17

Contraceptives

Reproduction is the Rule of Nature—Unknown

- Contraceptives.
- Combined monophasic pill: most commonly used (combination of estrogen and progestogen).
- **Triphasic combined pill:** Estrogen and progestogen but the ratio varies during the month to mimic the natural hormonal pattern in the menstrual cycle.
- **Progestogen only pill:** Mini pill.

Advantages of Combined Pills

- These are simple to use and highly effective.
- No special preparation is necessary before intercourse.
- The pill may relieve irregular menstrual periods, cramps and premenstrual tension.
- Less likely to get cancer of the uterus.
- Less suffering from ovarian cysts.
- Much less likely to suffer from ectopic pregnancy.
- Fewer attacks of rheumatoid arthritis.

Disadvantages

- Some women have difficulty remembering to take their daily pill.

- Some women experience side effects such as nausea, breast tenderness or, weight gain or loss, headache, depression and spotting or bleeding between menstrual periods.
- The estrogen -containing contraceptives present increased risk of serious disorders due to blood clotting in some women (low dose is recommended).
- A woman should not take the combined pill while breast -feeding an infant.
- Oral contraceptives sometimes interact with other drugs. This can result in diminished contraceptive effectiveness or interference with another drug's activity.
- Average annual failure rate including patient error and omissions: 2.6 unwanted pregnancies per 100 couples.

Progestogen Only Pill (Mini Pill)

- Has higher failure rate than combined pill.
- Suitable for lactating mother.
- Mechanism of action: These act by interfering with the passage of sperm through the cervical mucous, also affect the endometrium making it less suitable for implantation of the embryo.

Side Effects

- Headache
- Intermittent bleeding
- Hypertension.
- Nausea
- Thrombosis

Injectable Contraceptives

- Has proven to be highly effective method of fertility regulation.
- The most widely available injectable contraceptive in the U.K., Germany, New Zealand, Sweden and many countries all over the world.
- Contents: synthetic progesterone, administered once every three months.
- Side effects: headache, dizziness, weight gain, menstrual disturbances, no life threatening complications such as CV effects seen with Ocs.

Implants

- The recent development in the field of hormonal contraception.
- Six capsules which are implanted under the skin of the arm and provide contraception for five years.
- It should be put in the place by a trained health worker and at the end of the five years the capsules can be removed.

Unit 18

Emergency Drugs in Medical Practice

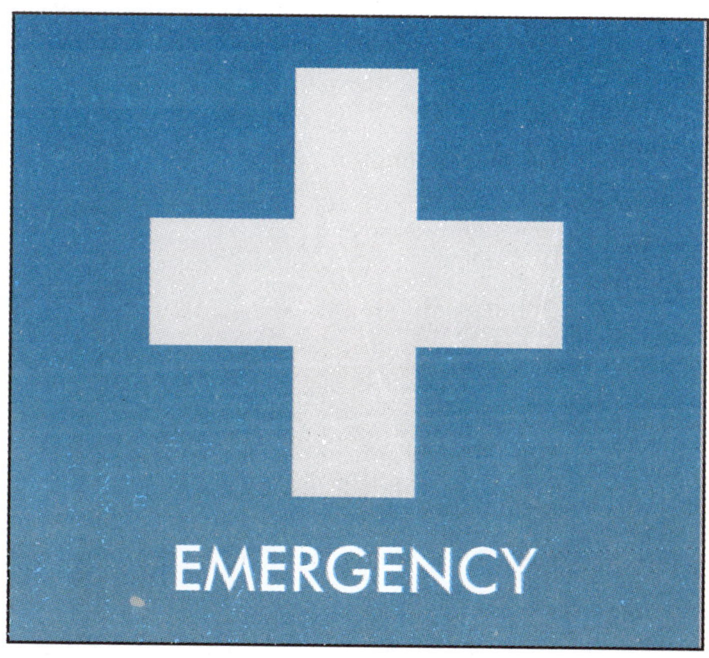

Urgent Situation need Immediate Response—Unknown

Several drugs are used in emergency room and intensive care units:

(a) Sedatives
  - Benzodiazpeines

(b) Analgesics
  - NSAIDS
  - Opioids

(c) Muscle Relaxants
  - Succinylcholine

(d) Cardiac
  - Dopamine
  - Dobutamine

(e) Vasopressors
  - Adrenaline
  - Noradrenaline
  - Methoxamine
  - Mephenteramine

SEDATIVES

- These drugs decrease anxiety and agitation, and provide amnesia
- Reduce patient-ventilator dysynchrony.

- Decrease respiratory muscle oxygen consumption, facilitate nursing care in seriously ill patients.
- May prolong mechanical ventilation and increase costs.

VASOPRESSOR AND CARDIAC STIMULANTS

ADRENALINE

- Stimulates alpha and beta-adrenergic receptors; low doses tend to produce predominantly beta-effects while higher doses tend to produce predominantly alpha-effects.
- Stimulation of beta1-receptors in the heart increases the rate and force of contraction, resulting in an increase in cardiac output.
- Stimulation of alpha1-receptor causes peripheral vasoconstriction, which increases the systolic BP.

Uses

- Low cardiac output states
- Cardiac arrest
- Anaphylaxis

Contraindications

- Before adequate intravascular volume replacement.

Administration

- **Dose:** 0.01-0.30 μg/kg/min IV infusion via a central vein or alternatively 0.2-0.5 ml SC/IM (0.5-1 ml of 1:1000 (0.5-1 mg) made up to 5 ml with sodium chloride 0.9%).

  Intravenously, a bolus dose of 10 ml 1 in 10 000 solution (1 mg) is given. Titrate dose according to HR, BP, cardiac output, presence of ectopic beats and urine output.

  In anaphylaxis, IV bolus: 0.5-1.0 ml 1 in 10,000 solution (50-100 μg), may be repeated as per needed basis, according to blood pressure.

Precautions

- In the absence of haemodynamic monitoring; do not connect to central vein lumen used for monitoring pressure (surge of drug during flushing of line) to adrenaline solutions.
- Incompatible with alkaline solutions, e.g., sodium bicarbonate, furosemide, phenytoin and enoximone.

Adverse Effects

- Arryhthmias
- Tachycardia
- Hypertension
- Worsening of myocardial ischaemia.

ATROPINE

Competitive antagonist of muscarinic receptors of acetylcholine.

Uses

- Sinus bradycardia; can increase heart rate in these patients.
- Reversal of muscarinic effects of anticholinesterases.
- Organophosphate poisoning.

Contraindications

- Complete heart block; local anesthestic action can worsen the same.

Administration

- The drug is given as 6 mg IV bolus, up to 3 mg for bradycardia but for organophosphate poisoning:

1-2 mg initially is given intravenously and, then further 1-2 mg every 30 min as per needed basis.

Precaution

- Slow IV injection of small doses 0.3 mg can cause bradycardia due to vagal stimulation.

Adverse effects

- Sedation, confusion.
- Dry mouth and blurred vision.
- Urinary retention.
- Tachycardia and arrhythmias.
- Fever; commonly seen in children.
- Atrial arrhythmias and atrioventricular dissociation (without significant cardiovascular symptoms).
- Dose more 5 mg results in restlessness and excitation, hallucinations, delirium and coma.
- Elderly (increase in risk of CNS side-effects).
- Child with fever (increases temperature).
- Acute myocardial ischaemia (tachycardia may cause worsening).
- Prostatic hypertrophy-urinary retention.
- Acute-angle glaucoma (increase in IOP occurs).

DOPAMINE

This is naturally occurring catecholamine acting directly on alpha, and beta1 receptors. The drug also stimulates dopamine receptors and indirectly releases noradrenaline. The dose dependent actions are given in the table.

Action	Dose
Increases renal and mesenteric blood flow by stimulating dopamine receptors. The renal blood flow results in GFR and renal sodium excretion.	0.5-2.5 μg/kg/min
Stimulate beta 1 receptors causing myocardial contractility, stroke volume and cardiac output.	2.5 and 10 μg/kg/min
Stimulates alpha receptors causing SVR, ↓ renal blood flow and potential for arrhythmias.	10 μg/kg/min

Administration

Dopamine-200 mg is made up to 50 ml glucose 5% or sodium chloride 0.9% (4000 μg/ml) solution and is given via a central vein via accurate infusion pump.

Reduce dosage if urine output decreases or there is increasing tachycardia or development of new arrhythmias.

Precautions

- Do not inject into peripheral vein (risk of extravasation); do not connect to central venin lumen used for monitoring pressure (surge of drug during flushing of line).
- The drug is incompatible with alkaline solutions, e.g., sodium bicarbonate, furosemide, phenytoin and enoximone.
- Discard the solution if cloudy, discoloured, or not freshly prepared.

Uses

- Septic shock
- Low cardiac output.

Contraindications

- Phaeochromocytoma
- Tachyarrhythmias or ventricular fibrillation.

Adverse Effects

- Ectopic beats
- Tachycardia
- Angina
- Gut ischaemia
- Vasoconstriction

DOBUTAMINE

- This is a synthetic catecholamine and is used extensively with or without dopamine.
- Dobutamine has predominant beta1 effects but minimally increases heart rate and increases force of contraction significantly.
- Mild beta-2 and alpha1 effects and decreases peripheral and pulmonary vascular resistance.
- Systolic BP may be increased because of the augmented cardiac output.
- Dobutamine has no specific effects on renal or splanchnic blood flow, but may increase renal blood flow due to an increase in cardiac output. This is an indirect action.

Action	Dose
Titrate dose according to HR, BP, cardiac output, presence of ectopic beats and urine output.	IV infusion→1-25 µg/kg/min via a central vein

Administration

The drug is given as 250 mg made up to 50ml glucose 5% or sodium chloride 0.9% (5000 µg/ml).

Precautions

- Avoid using in the absence of invasive cardiac monitoring.
- Do not connect to central vein lumen used for monitoring pressure (surge of drug during flushing of line).
- The drug is incompatible with alkaline solutions,v e.g., sodium bicarbonate,furosemide, phenytoin etc.

Uses

- Low cardiac output states.

Contraindications

- Idiopathic hypertrophic subaortic stenosis; cardiac output can increase but the drug blood will not go anwhere!

Administration

- Adverse effects
- Tachycardia
- Ectopic beats

Cautions

- Acute myocardial ischaemia or MI
- β-Blockers (may cause dobutamine to be less effective)

NORADRENALINE

- The drug has a predominant alpha^1 stimulant effect predominates over its beta^1 effect, raising the BP by increasing the systematic vascular resistance.
- It increases the myocardial oxygen requirement without increasing coronary blood flow.
- Noradrenaline reduces renal, hepatic and muscle blood flow, but in septic shock, noradrenaline may

increase renal blood flow and enhance urine production by increasing perfusion pressure.

Uses

- Septic shock, with low vascular resistance.

Contraindications

- Hypovolaemic shock (as there may already be vasoconstriction).
- Acute myocardial ischaemia or myocardial infarction.

Action	Dose
Initially start at a higher rate than intended, to increase the BP more rapidly, and then reduce rate.	Usual dose range: 0.01-0.4 ?g/kg/min IV infusion via a central vein

Administration

The drug is given as 4 mg injection, made up to 50 ml glucose 5% (80 μg/ml).

Precaution

- Avoid the drug in the absence of haemodynamic monitoring.

- Do not use a peripheral vein (risk of extravasation); also, do not connect to CVP lumen used for monitoring pressure (drug flushing).

Adverse Effects

- Bradycardia
- Hypertension
- Arrhythmias
- Myocardial ischaemia

Cautions

- Hypertension and heart disease(If extravasation of noradrenaline occurs; phentolamine an alpha blocker of non-selective type is given as 10 mg in 15 ml sodium chloride 0.9% should be infiltrated into the ischaemic area with a 23-G needle).

VASOPRESSIN

- Vasopressin (antidiuretic hormone, ADH) controls water excretion in kidneys via V_2 receptors. The drug causes constriction of vascular smooth muscle via V_1 receptors.

- In normal subjects vasopressin infusion has no effect on blood pressure but has been shown to significantly increase blood pressure in septic shock patients.

Action	Dose
In septic shock: reserve its use in cases where the noradrenaline dose needed is high	Upto 0.3 µg/kg/min
Cardiac arrest	40 unit

Contraindications

- Vascular disease, especially coronary artery disease.

Administration

- IV infusion: 1-4 units/h. The drug is diluted in in 20ml glucose 5% (1 unit/ml) and start at 1 unit/h,increasing to a maximum of 4 units/h (40 units -1ml ampoule))
- Do not stop the noradrenaline, as it works synergistically with vasopressin.

Adverse Effects

- Myocardial and peripheral ischaemia
- Hypertension

SUXAMETHONIUM

This is a Depolarising type of neuromuscular blocker.

This is the agent of choice for:

- Rapid tracheal intubation as part of a rapid sequence induction.
- Procedures requiring short periods of tracheal intubation, e.g.cardioversion.
- Management of severe post-extubation laryngospasm unresponsive to gentle positive pressure ventilation.

Contraindications

History of malignant hyperpyrexia (potent trigger).

Hyperkalaemia

Action	Dose
Rapid sequence intubation	1.0-1.5 mg/kg IV bolus

Adverse Effects

- Malignant hyperpyrexia
- Hyperkalaemia
- Increase in IOP and ICP
- Muscle pain
- Bradycardia
- Apnoea in pseudocholinesterase deficiency.

PHENYTOIN

Uses

- Status epileptics.
- Anticonvulsant prophylaxis in post-neurosurgical/ post traumatic patients.

Contraindications

- Do not use IV phenytoin in patients with heart blocks.

Action	Dose
Status epipepticus	15 mg/kg, give at a rate not 50 mg/min (20-30 min), followed by 100 mg every 8 hourly for maintenance
Oral/IV maintenance	200-600 mg/day

Precautions

- Rapid IV bolus is not recommended (hypotension, arrhythmias, CNS depression). Also Do not dissolve in solutions containing glucose.
- IM injection is not recommended as the absorption is slow and erratic.

Adverse Effects

- Nystagmus, ataxia and slurred speech are dose related side effects.
- Hypotension upon rapid IV injection.
- Gingival hyperplasia (long-term) by oral route.
- Rashes
- Folate deficiency megaloblastic anaemia

Cautions

- Metabolism subject to other enzyme inducers and inhibitors.

NALOXONE

- This is a specific opioid antagonist

Uses

- Reversal of opioid adverse effects - respiratory depression, sedation,pruritus and urinary retention.
- The drug is also used as a diagnostic test of opioid overdose in an unconscious patient.

Action	Dose
Reversal of opioid overdose	200 μg IV bolus, repeat every 2-3 min until desired response, up to a total of 2 mg
Reversal of spinal opioid-induced pruritus	Dilute 200 μg in 10 ml give 20 μg boluses every 5 min until symptoms resolve

Caution

- Titrate dose carefully in postoperative patients to avoid sudden return of severe pain.

Adverse Effects

- Arrhythmias and hypertension occurs.

LIDOCAINE

- Lidocaine is an anti-arrhythmic agent suppresses automaticity of conduction and spontaneous depolarisation of the ventricles.
- Clearance is related to both hepatic blood flow and hepatic function; it will be prolonged in liver disease, cardiac failure and the elderly
- The effects after the initial bolus dose last about 20 min.

IV infusion is needed to maintain the anti-arrhythmic effect.

Action	Dose
Ventricular arrhythmias	Loading dose of 1.5 mg/kg IV over 2 min, repeat after 5 min to a total dose of 3 mg/kg if necessary. Reduce dose in the elderly.
	Maintenance dose of 4 mg/min for 1st hour, 2 mg/min for 2nd hour and 1 mg/min thereafter. Reduce infusion rates in patients with hepatic impairment, cardiac failure and in the elderly.

Adverse effects

- Paraesthesia,muscle twitching, tinnitus are early side effects; confusion, convulsions can occur as well.
- Overdose can cause hypotension, bradycardia, asystole etc.

Precautions Cautions

- Decrease dose in hepatic impairment.
- Cardiac failure.

AMIODARONE

- This is broad spectrum anti-arrhythmic.
- This may result from its alpha- and beta-adrenoceptor-blocking properties as well as from its calcium channel-blocking effect in the coronary vessels.
- It causes minimal myocardial depression

Uses

- Ventricular and supraventricular arrhythmias, including those associated with WPW syndrome.

Action	Dose
Arrhythmias	150 mg over the FIRST - 10 minutes (15 mg/min) dilute with 5% dextrose.
	Slow: 360 mg over the next 6 hours at the rate of 1 mg/min.

Contraindications

- Iodine sensitivity (amiodarone contains iodine)
- Sinus bradycardia (risk of asystole)

Precautions

- Avoid with sodium chloride 0.9% and do not use via peripheral vein due t thrombophlebitis.

Adverse Effects

- Skin reactions.
- Vasodilation and hypotension or bradycardia after rapid infusion
- Pulmonary fibrosis, alveolitis and pneumonitis (usually reversible on stopping); most common long term problems.
- Liver dysfunction

- Hypo- or hyperthyroidism.
- Peripheral neuropathy

AMINOPHYLLINE

The drug is a ethylenediamine salt of theophylline.

- It is a commonly used bronchodilator for emergency use in asthma by IV route.
- Positive inotropic and chronotropic effects
- Diuresis

Uses

- Prevention and treatment of bronchospasm

Action	Dose
Bronchospasm	Loading dose: 5mg/kg IV, given over 30min, followed by maintenance dose 0.1-0.8mg/kg/h.

Adverse Effects

- Tachycardia
- Arrhythmias
- Convulsions

DIAZEPAM

This is a long acting benzodiazepine

Uses

- Termination of epileptic fit

Action	Dose
Status epilepticus	5-10 mg over 2 min, repeated if necessary after; 15 minutes, up to a total of 30 mg.

Precaution

Avoid the IM injection – painful and unpredictable absorption

Adverse effects

- Respiratory depression and apnoea.
- Sedation.

DIGOXIN

- This is a long acting anti-arrhythmic drug with inotropic properties.

- Digoxin is useful for controlling the ventricular response in AF and atrial flutter.
- Also useful in supraventrcular tachycardia.

Contraindications

- Intermittent complete heart block.
- Second-degree AV block.
- WPW syndrome.
- Hypertrophic obstructive cardiomyopathy.
- Constrictive pericarditis.

Administration

Action	Dose
Congestive heart failure with atrial fibrillation	IV loading dose: 0.5-1.0 mg in 50 ml glucose 5% or sodium chloride 0.9 %, given over 2 hours; Maintenance dose: 50-250 µg daily

Precautions

- Obtain periodic ECG.
- Serum digoxin level.
- IM injections not recommended

Adverse Effects

- Anorexia, nausea, vomiting
- Diarrhoea, abdominal pain
- Visual disturbances, headache
- Delirium, hallucinations
- Arrhythmias – all forms

FUROSEMIDE

This is a loop diuretic.

Uses

- Acute oliguric renal failure
- Pulmonary oedema

Action	Dose
Oliguric rebal failure; pulmonary edema	IV bolus:10-40mg over 3-5 min; IV infusion: 2-10 mg/h. For high-dose therapy (up to 1000 mg/day), dilute in 250-500 ml sodium chloride 0.9% given at a rate not 250 mg/h

Adverse Effects

- Hypovolumia, hypokalaemia,hypomagnesaemia
- Hyperuricaemia,hyperglycaemia
- Ototoxicity

PHENOBARBITAL SODIUM

Uses

- The drug is an option in status epilepticus.

Contraindications

- Porphyria.

Administration

Action	Dose
Status epilepticus	Phenobarbital can be continued at a rate of 50 mg/min until seizures cease; maximum cumulative dose in the absence of intubation, 20 mg/kg. Maintenance dose: 1 mg/kg IV 12 hourly.

POTASSIUM CHLORIDE

Uses

The drug is used in hypokalaemia.

Action	Dose
Hypokalemia correction	IV infusion: 20 mmol in 50 ml sodium chloride 0.9% or glucose 5% via central line or undiluted via central line

Precautions

- Monitor serum potassium regularly and check serum magnesium in refractory hypokalaemia
- NEVER use potassium chloride to reconstitute antibiotics as this has inadvertently caused several deaths.

Adverse Effects

- Muscle weakness
- Arrhythmias
- ECG changes.

PROPOFOL

Propofol is an IV anaesthetic induction agent or used as a sedative drug in the critically ill patients.

Sedation	Dose
	IV bolus between 10-20mg as per needed and IV infusion up to 4mg/kg/h.

How not to use Propofol

Do not exceed recommended dose range for sedation (up to 4 mg/kg/h)

Adverse Effects

- Hypotension
- Bradycardia
- Pain on injection.

SALBUTAMOL

Uses

- Reverses bronchospasm and is used in status asthmaticus.

Administration

Action	Dose
Reversing bronchospasm	2.5-5 mg 6 hourly, undiluted (if prolonged delivery time desirable then dilute with sodium chloride 0.9% only) given as a nebulized solution.

Adverse Effects

- Tremor, tachycardia

Unit 19

Miscellaneous Pharmacology

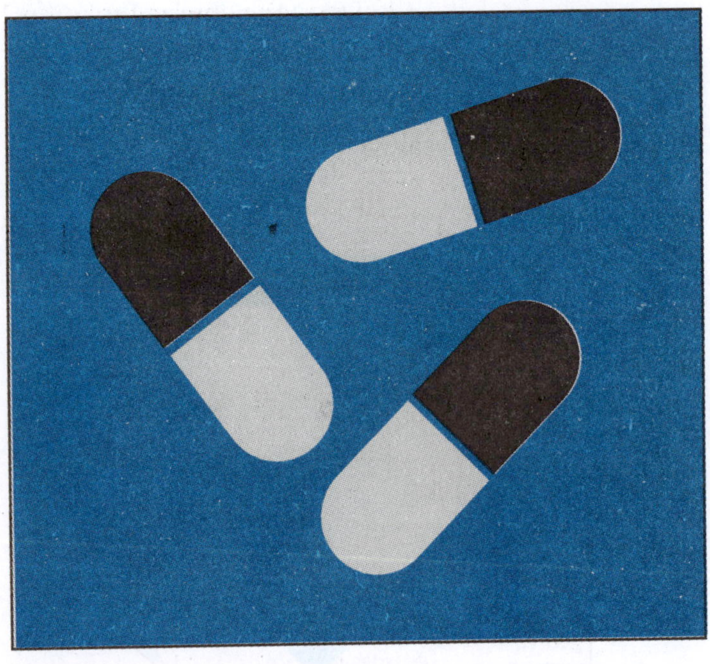

Medicines is learnt by errors

— William Oslar

DRUGS FOR ERECTILE DYSFUNCTION

- **Phosphodiaesterase inhibitors:** Drugs like sildenafil, verdenafil, tadalafil, udenafil and avanafil are drugs available to treat erectile dysfunction. Sildenafil types of drugs inhibit phosphodiaesterase-V isoform and increase nitric oxide, that stimulates cyclic GMP. Drugs cause hypotention as a side effects. Should be avoided with nitrates due to added risk of hypotension. Inhibition of phospho-diaesterase-VI can cause visual side effects as well. Sildenafil is a good pulmonary vasodilator and is used in primary pulmonary hypertension as well.

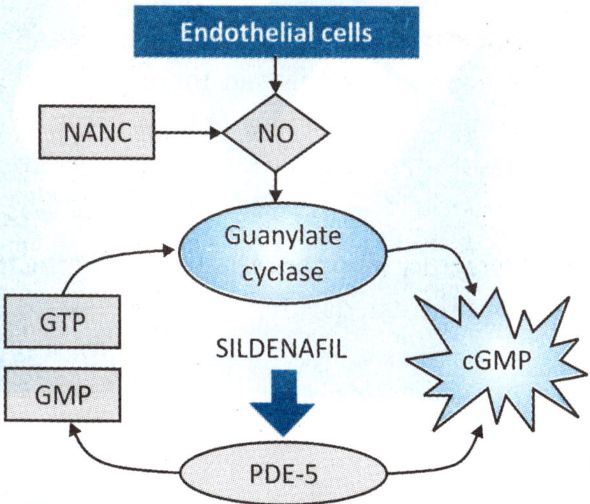

Figure: *Mechanism of action of sildenafil*

- **Dopamine agonists:** Apomorphine, bromocriptine are capable of stimulating dopamine receptors and hence can inhibit the release of prolactin. This may help to prevent hyperprolactinemia induced impotence.
- **Prostaglandin analogue:** Alprostadil is a prostaglandin analogue (PGE_1) that can dilate blood vessels of corpora cavernosa. The drug can produce penile erection in those who are otherwise not able to achieve significant erection by themselves. Repeat injections however should be avoided. This can cause penile fibrosis (Peyronie's disease).
- **Opioids:** Naltrexone is the most potent opioid antagonist and this can therefore reduce the action of endogenous opioids. High levels of these opioids can potentially interfere with normal libido and erectile ability.
- **Refractory impotence:** Impotence refractory to drugs is treated with penile prosthesis.

DRUGS FOR NEURODEGENERATIVE DISEASES

- **Anti-cholinesterases: Rivastigmine** has been the first drug to be used for the treatment of Alzheimer's disease. The drug acts by increasing the levels of acetylcholine in brain by inhibiting its degradation. Side effects include nausea, vomiting, abdominal pain etc. In patients who are not able to tolerate the drug due to its side effects, patch form is available. This has lesser risk of gastro-intestinal side effects. **Donepazil** is a safer version and is more potent. It is therefore considered to be the drug of choice for Alzheimer's disease. **Galantamine** is another anticholineterease. The drug has equal efficacy to that of donepazil.

- **NMDA receptor blocker:** NMDA receptors mediate cell mediated cytotoxicity inside brain cells. **Memantine** can be given for patients with moderate to severe Alzheimer's disease.

- **Anti-psychotics:** Drugs like risperidone and quetiapine are atypical antipsychotics that are used for short term management of patients with dementia. These can help to manage behavioural and psychological symptoms (BPSD). They should however not be used for long term as these can increase risk of stroke.

- **Anti-depressants:** Depression in dementia is common and can be confused with dementia per se. Therefore, depression needs to be treated. Drugs like citalopram or ecitalopram/sertraline are considered best for treating.
- **Anti-oxidants:** Vitamin E is an anti-oxidant and has extensively been investigated for patients with Alzheimer's disease. The drug has a potential to slow neurodegeneration in Alzheimer's disease. However, this is controversial.
- **Selegiline/rasigiline:** Drugs of this class have anti-oxidant activity and are mono-amine oxidase activity. Both of them have potential to slow down neuron loss in Parkinson's disease patients. However, this is not universally agreed upon.
- **Glutamate antagonists:** Glutamate is an abundant excitatory neurotransmitter in brain and the riluzole can block the effect. It is indicated in amyotropic lateral sclerosis. The drug can delay the need for tracheostomy or mechanical ventilation. It is highly expensive drug.

ANTI-OBESITY

- **Lipase inhibitors:** Orlistat is an inhibitor of pancreatic lipases, a group of enzymes degrading triacylglycerol in intestine. Steatorrhea is the major side effect.
- **Caninabinoid blockers:** Rimonabant is a blocker of CB1 receptors and has the ability to suppress appetite. The drug also has anti-smoking effect. Depression is a major side effect. It also has memory enhancing ability.
- **Sibutramine:** This is an amphetamine analogue and acts centrally. The drug reduces appetite and has now been withdrawn from market of many countries. Side effects include hypertension and cardiac valvular fibrosis.
- **Fenfluramine:** This is a similar drug and causes pulmonary hypertension and cardiac fibrosis.
- **Pramlintide:** This is an amyelin analogue and acts by reducing appetite. Drawback is that it needs to be injected at mealtime. It is used mainly for treatment of diabetes.

VITAMINS

- Iron is ubiquitous elemental compound that plays a vital role in carrying oxygen. This is used to correct iron deficiency anemia. Worms, malaria and ulcers are the common causes.
- Vitamins are broadly of two types: fat soluble and lipid soluble. ADEK are lipid soluble but vitamin B complex group vitamins are water soluble.
- Ascorbic acid or vitamin C can facilitate iron absorption and hence can help in correcting iron deficiency. Boiling can destroy this important vitamin. Since it is metabolized to oxalate, excessive consumption can cause renal stones of oxalate type.
- **Vitamin A:** Dairy products are rich sources of vitamin A; it is also found in carrots and green leafy vegetables. Retinal, retinol and retinoic acid are different forms of vitamin A. It is needed for cellular integrity, immune functions and growth and differentiation of epithelial functions. Deficiency can cause Bitot's spots, night blindness, xerosis and keratomalacia. Skin can also become rough and dry. There is increased risk of respiratory infections. Pseudo-tumor cerebri can occur due to overdose of vitamin A. Tretinoin, isotretinoin and acitretin are vitamin A analogues (retinoids) used in treatment of

refractory acne and severe psoriasis. All of these drugs have a high risk of teratogenicity, hence totally avoided in women with pregnancy. Tazoretene is used for treatment of psoriasis. Side effects include dry skin.

- **Vitamin D** is a hormone and acts via nuclear receptors like vitamin D. In association with parathyroid hormone, the major role of this hormone is regulate serum calcium. Reduced calcium and phosphate are seen in vitamin D deficiency. Reduced calcification of bones in children can cause rickets. Likewise, osteomalacia can occur in adults. Excess amount can cause renal stone formation.

- **Vitamin E** is found in good amounts in nuts (e.g., cashew nuts). Deficiency can cause increase RBC fragility.

- **Water soluble vitamins B_1:** Wheat, grain, yeasts and vegetables are rich sources. It serves as a coenzyme for catalyzing metabolic reactions in carbohydrate metabolism. Deficiency leads to peripheral neuritis and Beri-Beri, which has cardiovascular manifestations (e.g. CHF). Wernicke's encephalopathy involves CNS and include ataxia, nystagmus and opthalmoplegia. Korsakoff's psychosis includes memory disturbances (e.g., confabulations – false memories). 50-100 mg of thiamine can prevent encephalopathy in alcoholics with deficiency.

- **Riboflavin B_2:** Present in vegetables and non-vegetarian food and is a part of co-enzyme Q. B_2 plays a coenzyme role in flavin (e.g., FMN) mediated reactions. Angular stomatitis, cheilosis, glossitis are manifestations of deficiency.
- **B_3:** Niacin is present in vegetarian and non-vegetarian foods and plays a coenzyme role in NADP mediated reactions. Pellagra is a major manifestation of deficiency. Diarrhea, dermatitis and dementia can occur as a result of deficiency. High dose reduces VLDL levels and is used in management of dyslipidemias.
- **Pantothenic acid B_5** is a precursor of coenzyme A and plays an important role in synthesis of acetylcholine.
- **Pyridoxine B_6** is important coenzyme is metabolism of amino acids. Peripheral neuritis, seizures and anemia are manifestations of deficiency. INH, ethionamide, cycloserine, alcohol can cause deficiency symptoms. High doses for prolonged periods however should be avoided due to fear of toxic neuropathy. It is an antidose of INH and is also used in sideroblastic anemia.

Unit 20

Just Before Exam

Let food be thy medicine, and
medicine be thy food
— Hippocrates

GENERAL PHARMACOLOGY

1. MC mode of drug absorption is passive diffusion; lipid solubility is MC determinant.
2. **Vd** (Volume of distribution) is hypothetical volume in which the drug is distributed.
3. **Vd**=amount/plasma concentration.
4. *Clearance* is the volume of plasma that gets filtered of the drug in unit time.
5. Clarence (Cl)=rate of elimination/plasma concentration.
6. It is of two types–Zero order (amount constant) and First order (fraction constant).
7. Both half-life and Cl remain constant in first order kinetics while both change in zero order.
8. Half-life-time taken by the drug to reduce its concentration by half. A drug is eliminated completely in 4-5 half-lives.
9. It can tell about total duration of drug action and time to achieve plasma steady state concentration.
10. *Dose response curve* is the relationship between log of dose and response.
11. Slope indicates safety, X-axis indicates potency and height indicates efficacy.

12. Teratogens are drugs that cause teratogenicity; thalidomide is most potent teratogens (Phocomelia).
13. Thalidomide is now a days used as a TNF alpha blocker and is used in multiple myeloma.
14. *DOC for* epilepsy in pregnancy is *phenobarbitone*; typhoid fever is treated by ampicillin. However, resistant typhoid fever is treated by ceftriaxone.

AUTONOMIC NERVOUS SYSTEM

1. Botulinum toxin *reduces* release of acetylcholine used in *spasmodic disorders of muscles.*
2. Acetylcholine is metabolized by *true* (neuronal enzyme) and *false* pseudocholinesterase (deficiency causes apnea).
3. Bethanechol (direct acting cholinomimetic) is used in Hirsprung's disease, achalasia cardia and post-operative urinary retention.
4. *Neostigmine* is DOC for post-operative recovery from non-depolarizing blockers, cobra bite and myasthenia gravis.
5. DOC for *organophosphate poisoning* is atropine; cholinesterase re-activators, e.g., pralidoxime, obidoxime can also be used.
6. Atropine is C.I. in amanita muscaria poisoning.
7. Glycopyrrolate is atropine substitute specially useful for older patients undergoing surgery as it is more cardiostable. It is a tertiary amine and does not enter blood brain barrier as it is a quarternary amine.
8. Pipenzolate is used for infantile colic, while flevoxate is used for ureteric colic.

9. Hyosine butylbromide (Buscopan) is used commonly as anticholinergic drug for abdominal pain of spasmodic type.
10. Dicyclomine has both antiemetics and anti-motion sickness property.
11. Hyoscine (levo-scopolamine) is DOC for motion sickness and has amnesic properties (was used post World War-2 to produce amnesia).
12. Adrenaline is DOC for angioedema, anaphylactic shock, cardiac arrest. It reduces formation of aqeous humor and increases aqueous humor drainage (main mechanism).
13. *Isoproteranol* is DOC for heart block (Causes pure rise of systolic BP) and also for *torsa de depointes.*
14. *Mephenteramine* is DOC for short term rise of BP.
15. Dopamine is DOC for cardiogenic shock; acts on D_1 receptors in kidney (renal vasodilator).
16. *Dobutamine* (beta$_1$ agonist-does not act on dopamine receptors) is DOC for pump failure (e.g., following AMI, heart surgery).
17. Phenyleprine is the drug that produces mydriasis without cycloplegia.
18. Midodrine is DOC for postural hypotension.

19. Methylphenidate is DOC for attention deficit hyperkinetic disorders.
20. *Imipramine* is DOC for nocturnal enuresis due to its anticholinergic property.
21. Ephedrine is DOC for hypotension induced by spinal anesthesia.
22. Alpha-blockers are of two types (selective and non-selective).
23. *Prazocin, terazocin* are selective $alpha_1$ blockers that do not cause reflex tachycardia as they do not increase release of norepinephrine.
24. *First dose hypotension* is most side effect of alpha blockers; they do not increase lipid levels like beta-blockers-rather reduce them.

CARDIOVASCULAR DRUGS

1. Nitrates are the DOC of *initial choice* for all sorts of angina pain.
2. Nitrates act by delivering NO (nitric oxide) and are mainly venodilators.
3. Beta-blockers are contraindicated in variant angina (would cause unopposed vasospasm).
4. DOC for variant angina (also called Prinzmetal's angina) are CCBs.
5. MC side effect of nitrates is headache or postural hypotension (tolerance develop with nitrates on regular use).
6. DOC for hypertension with BPH is Terazocin/ Prazocin.
7. DOC for hypertension with angina is beta-blocker (Beta-blockers are DOC for HT in stressed patients and those with high rennin levels).
8. DOC for hypertension with diabetes/nephropathy or normal rennin hypertension is ACE inhibits (most common side effect-cough, also cause hyperkalemia, CI in bilateral renal artery stenosis.)
9. ACE inhibitors are now initial DOC for CHF, young patients with hypertension, normal renin hypertension.

10. *Alpha-blockers* of selective type (Prazocin, Terazocin) do not cause reflex tachycardia (non-selective type, e.g., phentolamine cause it).
11. Quinidine can increase plasma levels of digoxin by reducing its renal elimination.
12. Procainamide is MC drug causing drug induced SLE (kidney is NOT involved); it has little or no anticholinergic activity. Note that other members of this class, e.g., quinidine/disopyramide have high activity.
13. *Amiadarone* is the most efficacious, broadest spectrum and longest-acting ($t_{1/2}$=70 days) anti-arrhythmic drug. Its most common side effect is pulmonary fibrosis – it also causes hypothyroidism and hyperthyroidism.
14. Amiodarone causes fatty liver initially and later causes shrinkage leading to micronodular cirrhosis.
15. Bretylium is DOC for LA induced arrythmias-acts by *inhibiting* release of norepinephrine.
16. *Sotalol* is beta-blocker with K^+ channel blocking activity.
17. *Adenosine* is the shortest acting anti-arrhythmic drug ($t_{1/2}$=<10 seconds) and is DOC for paroxysmal supraventricular tachycardia.

18. Digoxin ($t_{1/2}$=24-36 h) is MC used cardiac glycoside, excreted unchanged from kidney. Therefore, CI in renal failure. Digitoxin ($t_{1/2}$=165 h) undergoes enetro-hepatic circulation and is safe in renal failure (CI in hepatic failure).
19. Digoxin acts by inhibiting **Na+K+ATPase** and therefore increases cardiac contractility; heart rate is NOT increased (rather, decreased due to AV block).
20. Digoxin is CI in obstructive cardiomyopathy, aortic stenosis, ventricular tachycardia, and partial heart block (it is safe in full heart block).
21. MC precipitating factor of digoxin toxicity is hypokalemia (hyperkalemia is protective).
22. DOC for digoxin toxicity is potassium (CI in overdose).
23. DOC for overdose of digoxin toxicity is DIGIBIND (Fc fragment of digoxin binding antibody).
24. Esmolol is shortest acting beta-blocker ($t_{1/2}$=<10 minutes); metabolized in plasma therefore is safe in renal/hepatic failure (**Nadolol** is longest acting beta-blocker).
25. Sincere ANS (Nadolol, Atenolol, Sotalol) are water soluble beta-blockers and are excreted unchanged (CI in renal failure).

26. PALM (Propranolol, Pindolol, Acebutolol, Labetalol, Metoprolol) are beta-blockers with local anesthetic activity.
27. MC side effect of beta-blockers is bradycardia, they can also cause AV nodal block, depression, suicidal tendencies, nightmares, hyperlipidemia, impotence and worsening of asthma, diabetes and peripheral vascular disease. All non-selective blockers (propranolol, sotalol, nandolol, and timolol) are CI in pregnancy while cardioselective (atenolol, metoprolol, bisoprolol, betaxalol and esmolol) are safe in pregnancy.
28. Beta-blockers with ISA (alprenolol, oxprenolol, pindolol, carteolol, celiprolol, penbutolol) have NO adverse effect on lipid profile and they do not cause bradycardia.
29. Carvedilol (antioxidant property), labetalol (DOC for aortic dissection) and dilevalol are combined acting beta-blockers. Carvedolol is the DOC for cardioprotection in CHF.
30. Statins are MC used hypolipidemic drugs (others are fibric acid derivatives-clofibrate, fenofibrate, niacin, bile acid derivatives-cholestyramine, colistipol).
31. Statins (atorvastatin, Lovastatin (prodrug), Simvastatin (prodrug), prastatin) are inhibitors of

HMG CoA reductase (LDL receptor overexpression occurs-seen also with bile acid binding resins).

32. MC side effect of statins is increase in CPK (10% cases), many have muscle pain or *myoglobinurea.*
33. MC side effect of nicotinic acid is flushing-also causes hyperuricemia (only drug to increase HLD levels).

RENAL DRUGS

1. Thiazides (Act on early DCT) are DOC for hypertension as they act slowly and conserve calcium (useful in osteoporosis) they are DOC for hypertension diabetes insipidus, Liddle's syndrome, idiopathic hypercalciuria.
2. Thiazides (Hydrochlorothiazide is MC used) except metolazone and indapamide (undergo enterohepatic circulation) are unsafe in renal failure.
3. Furosemide (Act on Loop of Hanle (Na^+K^+2Cl) also sometimes called Tamm Horsfall protein) is the fastest acting (also called high ceiling diuretic).
4. MC side effect of both thiazides and furosemide is hypokalemia; furosemide can also cause volume depletion.
5. *Hypokalemia* is MC precipitating factor of digoxin toxicity (hyperkalemia prevents it).
6. *Spironolactone* (K^+ sparing diuretic) is DOC for refractory ascites; MC side effect is hyperkalemia. Spironolactone is a prodrug, forms canrenonone and is eliminated in urine. Therefore is contraindicated in renal failure. It does not require accesses to tubular lumen for its action. The drug

acts on collecting duct to block action of aldosterone.

7. Amiloride, triamterene are other K^+ sparing diuretics; these act at late distal convoluted tubules.
8. Mannitol is osmotic diuretic and is DOC for brain edema (not in intracerebral hemorrhage).
9. It can cause hyperkalemia, pulmonary edema and CI in established renal failure. This is because it can cause expansion of plasma volume.
10. *Demeclocycline* and *lithium* are ADH receptor antagonists, used in syndrome of inappropriate ADH secretion (also called as anti-diuretic).

DRUGS FOR CENTRAL NERVOUS SYSTEM DISEASES

1. Benzodiazepines are MC used sedatives and hypnotics. These are GABA facilitory drugs. Diazepam is MC used sedative and hypnotic with $t_{1/2}$-100; it is DOC for status epileptics, febrile seizures, drug induced hyperactivity, picrotoxin poisoning, prevention of seizures due to lidocaine, emergence delirium due to ketamine, drug induced EPS or excitement of mania-flumazenil is antidote of diazepam.
2. LEO (**L**orazepam, **E**stazolam, **Oxazepam**) are water-soluble benzodiazepines and are metabolized outside liver.
3. Benzodiazepines cause *anterograde amnesia* (head injury causes retrograde amnesia).
4. Chlordiazepoxide (high dose) is DOC for alcohol withdrawal from alcohol; diazepam is however for delirium *tremons.*
5. Flunitrazepam is *date rape drug*; chloral hydrate (dry wine), ketamine and GHB are other drugs for same purpose.
6. *Phenytoin* acts by inhibiting depolarizing shift in neurons; MC side effect is gum hyperplasia; others are hirsutism, hypocalcemia, osteomalacia,

megaloblastic anemia (do MCV testing), pseudolymphoma and hypersensitivity (discontinue the drug).

7. *Carbamazepine* is DOC for all kind of neuralgias (trigeminal/glossopharyngeal) and partial seizure; MC side effect is rash (10%), leukopenia and hepatitis.
8. *Valproic acid* is broadest spectrum antiepileptic drug; DOC for GTCS, akinetic, atonic, myoclonic and mixed epilepsies; causes hepatotoxicity mainly in children, weight gain.
9. *Phenobarbitone* is CI in acute intermittent porphyria; DOC for hemolytic anemia, jaundice in newborn, epilepsy following febrile seizures, and epilepsy in pregnancy.
10. *Buspirone* is a non-sedative anxiolytic drug ($5HT_{1A}$ partial agonist) that is devoid of properties that are there with diazepam such as muscular relaxation, amnesia, sedation, anti-convulsant action etc. Its main drawback is that it takes two weeks to start its action therefore is used in maintenance of patients with generalized anxiety disorders rather than in acute phase.
11. Thiopentone is highly lipid soluble (MC inducing agent), barbiturate that undergoes redistribution.

12. *Donepazil* is the DOC for Alzhiemer's disease, a organic brain disease (MC cause of dementia); occurs due to acetylcholine deficiency.
13. *Levodopa* is most effective anti-Parkinson drug, only drug that lowers mortality.
14. *Amantidine* (also an antiviral drug-Influenza A2) enhances dopamine transmission (MC side effect is ankle edema) CI in renal failure and epilepsy.
15. Tolcapone and entacapone are COMT inhibitors and are used in severe Parkinson's disease. Tolcapone can cause hepatic failure but is more potent.
16. *Morphine* was isolated by Serturner from poppy plant it is analgesic and antitussive.
17. *Pethidine* is synthetic opioid that has anticholinergic property (causes mydriasis) while other opioids cause meiosis.
18. Pethidine gets accumulated in renal failure causing hyperreflexia; this is known as norpethidine syndrome.
19. *Buprenorphine* is the longest acting opioid that has alcohol anti-craving properties (methadone is DOC for opioid detoxification). Importantly, buprenorphine binds to mu receptors so tightly that even morphine is not able to reverse its actions.

20. *Naloxone* (most potent opioid antagonist) does not reverse the overdose of Buprenorphine due to its ceiling effect.
21. Morphine is DOC for acute pulmonary edema, Tetralogy of Fellot's.
22. Opioids do not have anti-inflammatory properties but are useful in severe pain of visceral origin as they work by reducing the release of substance P from spinal cord's substantia gelatinososa.
23. Histamine's maximum amount is found in lung mast cells (90% of body's histamine is present there).
24. Astemazole is longest acting newer antihistaminic and citirizine, although a member of newer non-sedative family; out of newer drugs it produces maximum sedation. It has anti prion activity.
25. Older anti-histaminic are better for urticaria and itching due to their anticholinergic effects while newer ones are better for sneezing and common cold etc.
26. Fexofenadine (Allergra), a newer analogue of hepatotoxic and cardiotoxic drug terfenadine is not associated with torsa de depointes.
27. Citirizine is a metabolite of Promethazine but is devoid of sedative effect at usual therapeutic doses (in some it produces sedation).

28. Promethazine (phenargan) is DOC for drug induced extrapyramidal disturbances.
29. Sumatriptan, a 5-$HT_{1b/1d}$ partial agonist is the DOC for acute attack of migraine; propranolol is DOC for prevention of migraine.
30. Sumatriptan can cause vasospasm, therefore is contraindicated in hypertension, angina and peripheral vascular diseases patients.
31. Alcohol is most prevalent neurotoxin in our environment.
32. *Disulfiram* (metronidazole has disulfiram like effect) has is alcohol dehydrogenase inhibitor and is DOC for alcohol detoxification. It is being studied for cocaine dependence as well.
33. Legal limit of alcohol is 80 mg/dl in most nations and levels above 400 mg/dl are uniformly fatal; it follows zero order kinetics (phenytoin, tolbutamide, theophylline, warfarin, aspirin, caffeine) also follow zero-order kinetics (fixed amount is metabolized.
34. *Ethylene glycol* poisoning shows presence of oxalate crystals in urine.
35. *Fomepizole*/ethanol are DOC for methylalcohol poisoning (causes blindness due to optic atrophy).

NON-STEROIDAL ANTI-INFLAMMATORY DRUGS, ANTIGOUT, DMARDS AND AUTACOIDS

1. Aspirin is most commonly used NSAID, it has analgesic, antipyretic, antiinflammatory, anti-platelet and uricosuric actions.
2. Aspirin is contraindicated in ulcer patients, bleeding disorders, patients with nasal polyp, asthma and children with viral fever (Due to fear of Reye's syndrome-metabolic encephalopathy).
3. Aspirin is longest acting anti-platelet drug acting for more than 72 hours; its antiplatelet in low doses.
4. In aspirin poisoning; metabolic acidosis is seen in children while metabolic alkalosis is seen in adults.
5. Vitamin K and fresh frozen plasma are used in aspirin poisoning.
6. *Ibuprofen* is safest oldest NSAID but causes toxic amblyopia.
7. *Indomethacin* is long acting NSAID; MC side effect is frontal headache (50% cases); it is DOC for ankylosing spondylitis, acute gout, post-coital headache, Barter's syndrome and closure of PDA– it is contraindicated in drivers, machinery opera-

tors, hematological, neurological and psychiatrically ill patients.

8. COX-2 inhibitors (Celecoxib, rofecoxib, valdycoxib, parecoxib etc.) are safer newer NSAID with less likelihood of symptomatic GI side effects such dyspepsia, ulcer, heartburn etc.
9. *H. pylori* is MC cause of peptic ulcers; NSAIDs are 2nd MC cause-NSAID induced ulcers are H. pylori negative.
10. PGE_2 is a bronchodilator prostaglandin; others are bronchoconstrictor.
11. *PGE_1* (Misoprostol) used in ulcer prevention and maintenance of patency of ductus arterious but causes diarrhoea as MC side effect.
12. *$PGF_{2\ alpha}$* is a vasoconstrictor of pulmonary vessels, and is also used in post-partal hemorrhage and 2nd trimester abortions.
13. *Probenecid* and sulfinpyrazone are uricosuric drugs.
14. Allopurinol (Xanthine oxidase inhibitor) is used in chronic gout, hyper-uriacemia due to anticancer drugs, and those with gout and renal failure.
15. *Methotrexate* is MC used DMARD; bone marrow suppression and hepatic fibrosis are MC side effects; it is DHFR inhibitor, anti-folate.
16. Cyclosporine, an immunosuppressive drug is used as DMARD, causes hepato, nephrotoxicity but does not suppress bone marrow.

ANTIBIOTICS

1. All antibiotics acting by inhibiting protein synthesis other than tetracycline act by inhibiting 50-S ribosomal inhibition.
2. *Tetracycline* cause deformities of bones and teeth (maximum damage between, 3-6 years) CI, pregnancy, lactation and children below 8 years.
3. *Tigecycline* is a newer tetracycline and is eliminated by bile. It is effective against MRSA, VRSA.
4. *Doxycycline* and demeclocycline cause photosensitivity.
5. *Chloramphenicol* causes gray baby syndrome which occurs due to defective glucoronidation.
6. *Erythromycin* is MC used macrolides that causes diarrhea and hepatitis (more in pregnant women-specially estolate salt); acts on motilin receptors, increase intestinal motility.
7. *Fluroqunolones* such as ciprofloxacin (has anti-pseudomonal activity) are used in typhoid fever but damage growing cartilages; therefore are avoided in children <17 year age.
8. Gatifloxacin and sparfloxacin prolong QT interval and trofloxacin cause hepatitis.
9. *Levofloxacin* and *pefloxacin* cause photosensitivity.

10. *Sulphonamides* are contraindicated in newborns because they cause jaundice due to albumin displacement.
11. Vancomycin is DOC for MRSA, causes ototoxicity, nephrotoxicity, MC side effect is Red Man Syndrome.
12. Cotrimoxazole act by sequential blockade, and is the DOC for *pneumocystic carnii*, Whipple's disease and nocardiosis.
13. *Spiramycin* is DOC for toxoplasmosis in pregnancy.
14. *Sulfadiazine*+pyrimethamine is DOC in non-pregnant women.
15. *Fluoroquinolones* inhibit DNA gyrase (topisomerase-2), and damage cartilages (CI children <17 yr.).
16. *Levofloxacin* and *Pefloxacin* cause photosensitivity.
17. *Methicillin* causes interstitial nephritis, acid labile.
18. Methoxypenicllin (Penicllin V) is acid stable, given orally.
19. Penicillins are excreted unchanged by tubular filtration.
20. Probenacid can be given to prolong their duration.

21. Ampicillin causes rashes in patients with infectious mononucleosis and with allopurinol.
22. MC side effect of ampicillin is diarrhea.
23. Ampicillin is DOC for listeria meningitis.
24. Imipenem is DOC for eneterobacter and is broadest spectrum antibiotic of penicillin class.
25. Ceftriaxone is the longest acting cephalosporin and is DOC for *H. influenza,* meningitis (except listeria), gonorrhea and typhoid fever. It is partly eliminated by bile. Another antibiotic of generation-III eliminated partly by bile is cefoparamide. Note that cefoperazone is eliminated totally by bile.
26. Aminoglycosides are *ototoxic* and *nephrotoxic*-Gentamicin is most nephrotoxic, while streptomycin is most *vestibultoxic* antibiotic.
27. Aminoglycosides cause misreading of t-RNA-amino acid complex and premature termination of chain elongation
28. Amphotericin-B is DOC for invasive or systemic fungal infections; causes hypokalemia, nephro-toxicity and hypersensitivity (test dose is needed).
29. Amp B causes both hypo and hyperkalemia and can also cause significant nephrotoxicity. An important feature of drug is *hypo-magnesemia*. Note

that furesemide too can cause significant *hypomagnesemia*.

30. Itracnazole is DOC for blastomycosis, and Fluconazole for cryptococcal meningitis (can cause hypokalemia). It is a weak enzyme inhibitor; however, saquinavir, a protease inhibitor is weaker than itraconazole.
31. *Griseofulvin* (inhibits microtubules) is DOC for systemic dermatophytoses, due to low efficacy, its been replaced by terbinafine in onychomycosis.
32. *Nevaripine+Zidovudine* combination is used to reduce maternal to fetal transmission.
33. *Zidovudine+lamividuine* is used following accidental needle injury while drawing blood from HIV positive patient.
34. *Lamividuine* (DOC for HBV) does NOT cause neuropathy while Stavudine (MC drug), zalcitabine, diadanosine cause peripheran neuropathy. Indinavir causes renal stones and is MC drug causing lipodystrophy.
35. HIV protease inhibitors (Nelfinavir, squinavir, amprenavir, lopinavir, ritonavir and indinavir etc.) should not be used with rifampin.
36. *Rifabutin* can safely be used with HIV protease inhibitors.

37. MC side effect of zidovudine is anemia (avoid with paracetamol as it can interfere with its metabolism).
38. *Amantadine* is antiviral with anti-Parkinson activity; ankle edema is MC side effect and is CI in epilepsy and renal failure.
39. *Chloroquine* is DOC for prophylaxis, malaria in pregnancy and vivax malaria.
40. *Quinine* is DOC for severe falciparum malaria. MC side effect is hypoglycemia.
41. *Mefloquine* prolongs QT interval and is contraindicated in heart block, psychiatric and epileptic patients.
42. *Artemisinin* derivatives (artether, artemether) are fastest acting anti-malarial drugs used in severe and resistant malaria.
43. *Metronidazole* is DOC for giardiasis, amoebiasis (hepatic and intestinal), trichomonas vaginalis and gardnerella vaginalis (MC-S/E nausea, metallic taste, disulfiram like reaction).
44. *Diloxanide furate* is DOC for asymptotic cyst passers.
45. *Emetine/Dehydroemetine* are used in serious cases with hepatic Amoebiasis but are cardiotoxic.

46. INH is most rapidly acting ATT, acts on both intra and extracellular bacterial penetration into caseous material is best; peripheral neuropathy (prevented by B_6) is MC side effect, also hepatitis.
47. Mutation in INH_A gene/KatG gene can give rise to resistance in case of INH.
48. *Rifampin* is slowly acting ATT, acts on intermittent growers and spurters-can sterilize cavities, cause organish red coloration, inhibits DNA dependent DNA polymerase hepatitis.
49. If given once a month or fortnightly, rifampin produces more s/e such as cutaneous syndrome, abdominal syndrome, flu like syndrome.
50. *Ethambutol* is not metabolized, excreted unchanged, causes interference of red-green vision (optic neuritis–MC serious s/e), and is CI in children below 6 years. Note that the drug is NOT hepatotoxic.
51. *Pyrazinamide* causes hepatitis, hyperuricemia (aspirin can be used), and is slowly acting bactericidal ATT-has cavity sterilizing activity.
52. *Streptomycin* is bacteriostatic ATT with oto and nephrotoxicity.

53. *Dapsone* is DOC for leprosy, anemia (mostly hemolytic) is MC side effect; also methemoglobinemia, megaloblastic anemia (as it is antifolate drug).
54. *Melarsoprol* is DOC for CNS stage of African trypanosomiasis.
55. *Suramin* is DOC for hemolymphatic stage of African trypanosomiasis.
56. *Nifurtimox* is DOC for American trypanosomiasis.
57. *Sodium stibogluconate* is DOC for leishmaniasis (both visceral and cutaneous).
58. *Pentamidine* is used in resistant cases with visceral leishmaniasis; but causes hypotension, and pancreatitis (diabetes may be permanent).
59. *Miltefostine* is most effective drug against leishmaniasis; also is the safest drug for leishmania discovered so far.
60. *Albendazole* is DOC for all nematodes helminthic infections except Strongyloides (ivermectin is DOC), *W. bancrofti* (DEC is DOC) and Oncocerchiasis (ivermectin is DOC).
61. *Albendazole* is the DOC for neurocysticercosis. Though, praziquantel can also be used but is NOT the DOC.

GASTROINTESTINAL DRUGS

1. *Apomorphine* is used to produce vomiting in poisoning via parenteral route, while *ipecacuhana* via oral route.
2. Induction of vomiting is contraindicated in kerosene poisoning, acid and alkali poisoning-due to fear of aspiration and perforation.
3. *Metochlopramide* is MC used antiemetics but is D_2 blocker, therefore causes hyper-prolactinemia, and extrapyramidal side effects. It is DOC for aspiration phneumonitis (also called as Mendelson's syndrome).
4. Domperidone blocks D_2 receptors only in CTZ center and not in basal ganglia, therefore does not cause EPS (can even be used in Parkinson patients).
5. *Cisapride* is a promotility (prokinetic or motility enhancing) drug with no antiemetics activity.
6. *Cisapride* given with enzyme inhibitors such as erythromycin, azoles, ciprofloxacin can cause *torsa de depointes.*
7. *Mosapride*, itopride etc. are free from *torsa de depointes* effect.

8. *Cimetidine* is the oldest and most toxic H_2 blocker (causes gynecomastia and taste disturbances-dysgusia-ACE I also cause it).
9. *Ranitidine* is free from gynaecomastia.
10. Antacids are fast acting anti-ulcer drugs but relapse rate is high-aluminum containing antacids cause constipation and intestinal obstruction.
11. Aluminum phosphate is used as a phosphate binder in CRF.
12. Magnesium oxide (milk of magnesia) cause diarrhea.
13. *Omeprazole*, rabeprazole, esomeprazole, pentaprazole etc. drugs are PPIs and are DOCs for all acid related conditions (e.g., dyspepsia, ulcers, reflux esophagitis, Zollinger Ellison's syndrome).
14. They are safe drug and MC side effect is hypergastreniemia.
15. *Misoprostol* (PGE_1) is an ulcer protective drug; previously, it was DOC for NSAID induced ulcers now PPIs are DOCs.
16. *Bismuth subcitrate*, de-glycerinized liquorice (has mineralocorticoid effectaldosterone like effect) are ulcer healing drugs; bismuth has anit-H. pylori activity but can cause encehpahlopathy and osteodystrophy.

17. Metronidazole, clarithromycin/ampicillin/PPI are combination therapy (triple therapy) for eradication of *H. pylori.*
18. *Loperamide* (a synthetic opioid–LOMOTIL) is the DOC for functional diarrhoea (non-infectious, e.g., travelers diarrhoea) it is free from disadvantages of opioids, e.g., respiratory depression as it does not enter BBB.
19. *Diphenoxylate* (Lomofen) is combination of atropine + Loperamide.
20. Physillium, bran are bulk laxatives-form bulk induce laxative effect.
21. *Lactulose* is osmotic laxative-used in hepatic encephalopathy.
22. PEG (polyethylene glycol) solution is used to clean bowel for colonoscopies.
23. Colistipol/cholestyramine are used for bile acid induced diarrhoea.
24. DOSSS (dictylsodium sulphosuccinate) is detergent like drug for used for softening stool. Bisacodyl is also a laxative.
25. Cotrixmoxazole/fluoroquinolones are antibiotics used in Shigella dysentery; otherwise antibiotics are avoided in diarrheas.

26. Daptomycin (Protein synthesis inhibitor), tigecycline (Antibiotic of tetracycline class), delbavancin (long acting antibiotic), vancomycin, linezolid, teichoplanin, cotrimoxazole, ciprofloxacin, streptogramins (dalfoprisin + quinupristin) ceftobiprole (5th generation cephalosporin) are antibiotics against MRSA.

RESPIRATORY PHARMACOLOGY

1. Dry cough is suppressed (codeine, dextromethorphan), while wet cough is encouraged (with expectorant).
2. Bromhexine is MC mucolytic-rhinorrhoea/ lacrymation is MC side effect.
3. DOC of initial choice in bronchial asthma is inhaled beta-2 agonist.
4. Corticosteroid are used for persistent asthma.
5. Theophylline is a methylxanthines (inhibits PDE); increases cAMP in smooth muscles – it is a bronchodilator used for poorly controlled asthma.
6. MC side effect of theophylline is tremor–more common with ciprofloxacin or erythromycin-seizures, hyperreflexia occur in high doses–DOC for apnea in newborn.
7. Chromyglycate sodium is a mast cell stabilizer (not absorbed orally) and is DOC for prevention of exercise induced asthma.
8. Zileuton, zafirlekast, montelukast (not used in acute asthma) are used for aspirin- induced asthma.
9. Ipratropium bromide is DOC for COPD; anticholinergic drug causes dry mouth fungal infections can occur-nystatin is used.
10. Ketotifen is serotonin antagonist used for asthma prevention; chromoglycate however is the drug of choice for exercise induced asthma.

COAGULANT AND ANTI-COAGULANTS

1. Vitamin K is DOC for warfarin overdose, aspirin poisoning (used with fresh frozen plasma and acts by increasing synthesis of factor II, VII, IX, X).
2. MC side effect of vitamin K is fluishing (K1 MC used) K3, CI in newborn due to hemolytic jaundice.
3. *Warfarin* is MC used oral anticoagulant, acts by inhibiting synthesis of factor II, VII, IX, X.
4. MC side effect is bleeding but also cause fat and breast necrosis which is more common in patients with protein C or proteins S deficiency.
5. Anticoagulants (both heparin and warfarin) cause osteopenia and osteoporosis because they inhibit carboxylation of protein osteonectin.
6. *Heparins* (*hepa*: greek–from liver–discovered by McLean) are of 3 types physiological (e.g., danapranoid), low molecular weight (Mol. wt. <5000), e.g., enoxaparin, tinzaparin, dalteparin and high molecular weight (Mol. wt. > 10,000 e.g., Hirudin).
7. Heparin is CI in patients with active tuberculosis, bleeding peptic ulcers, bleeding disorders, intracranial hemorrhage, ocular surgery, *do not do lumber puncture in heparinized patients.*

8. MC side effect of heparins is bleeding; MC initial manifestation is hematuria; long term side effects include clotting, thrombocytopenia, osteoporosis, alopacia.
9. Heparin damages the platelets therefore the injured platelets clot together leading to formation of clot (white clot – as it is formed only by platelets).
10. LMWH are better because of better pharmacokinetics, once a day daily dosing, less chance of bleeding or clotting leading to embolism.
11. DOC for heparin overdose is *protamine sulphate*, which is a basic LMWH heparin by itself (1 mg-100 IU of heparin).
12. Fibrinolytic inhibitors (also called as antiplasmin drugs) such as tranhexaenemic acid, epsilon amnocaproic acid, and iprotinin are used in massive bleeding.
13. Thrombolytic drugs such streptokinase (DOC for AMI) act by converting plasminogen to plasmin, which inturn degrades clots.
14. MC side effect of streptokinase is hypotension-antibodies can reduce its effectiveness.
15. Urokinase and t-PA are direct plasminogen activators (do not evoke antibodies), anistrepplase is

longest acting (1-2 hours), streptokinase (20 min) and alteplase, retiplase (<10 min).

16. Bleeding is MC side effect – intracranial hemorrhage is most serious complication – they are contraindicated in *active bleed* (e.g., ulcer).

ENDOCRANIAL DRUGS

1. GnRH analogues (naferlin, goserlin, buserlin) are DOCs to suppress gonadotrophins secretion in precocious puberty, prostatic cancer, endometriosis, and fibroid uterus.
2. Mode of administration of GnRH analogues can determine their use.
3. Bromocriptine (partial agonist of D_1 receptors) is DOC for suppression of wanted lactation, hyperprolactenemia, acromegaly (carbergoline in pregnancy).
4. Somatrem/somatropin are growth hormone analogues used in short stature patients, e.g., Turner's syndrome (XO).
5. Cosyntropin (ACTH analogue) is DOC for infantile spasm.
6. Menotropins (FHS and LH) are used in hypogonadal states.
7. Oxytocin is used to induce or augment labour; CI renal failure, or hypertension with IHD.
8. *Desmopressin* (V2 agonist) is DOC for craniogenic diabetes insipidus; also useful in hemophilia and Von Willebrand's disease.
9. Hydrocortisone (DOC for CAH, acute and chronic adrenal insufficiency) is MC Glucocorticoid se-

creted endogenously (10 mg/day) while aldosterone is most potent mineralocorticoid (even up to 30 times more potent than fludrocortisone).

10. *Dexamethasone* has maximum topical activity while hydrocortisone has no topical activity.
11. Dexamethasone/betamethasone are longest acting Glucocorticoids (act for >24-36 hours); have no salt retaining activity but have maximum anti-inflammatory activity.
12. Des-oxy-corticosterone acetate has no glucocorticoids and is pure mineralocorticoid.
13. Thyroxine (less active), T3 (more active) are DOCs for myxedema, cretinism (usual dose is 25 microgram/day).
14. *Thionamides* (propylthiouracil, carbamezole etc. methimazole) are antithyroid drugs acting by inhibiting thyroid hormone synthesis (thyroid peroxides).
15. Propylthiouracil is least potent and shortest acting anti-thyroid drug (DOC for hyperthyroidism in pregnancy and thyroid storm).
16. MC serious side effect of anti-thyroid drugs is *agranulocytosis* (indicated by sore throat or fever-withdraw the drug).

17. *Lugol's iodine* acts by inhibiting release of thyroid hormones (DOC for making gland firm before surgery).
18. Radioactive iodine (I^{131} acts by delivering beta and gamma rays); destroys thyroid gland and is CI in young patients.
19. *Propranolol* is DOC of initial choice for toxic multinodular goiter.
20. Insulin is a polypeptide with mol. weight (5000) acting by tyrosine kinase receptors (autophosphorylation receptors). Benting and Best discovered it.
21. Inhibits phosphoenolcarboxykinase, phosphorylase (muscle and liver); stimulates hexokinase and lipoprotein lipase (LPL).
22. MC side effect is hypoglycemia, beta-blockers can cause silent hypoglycemia as they can block sympathetic manifestations of hypoglycemia.
23. Human insulin causes lipodystrophy; zinc is added to insulin to increase shelf-life and stability of solution.
24. Insulin lipspro is shortest acting while *insulin glargine* is longest acting.
25. Insulin Glarzine is an acidic insulin and therefore becomes polymerized upon injection into subcu-

taneous tissues. This ensures slow and sustained delivery of drug into circulation. Therefore, it is longest acting insulin.

26. *Sulphonylureas* increase insulin release also increase insulin sensitivity.
27. Tolbutamide is safest sulphonylureas, while chlorpropamide is worse (hypoglycemia is most likely, causes SIADH, disulfiram like reaction).
28. Glimepride is most potent and longest acting sulphonylureas.
29. Bigunides (Metformin and phenformin) act by inhibiting hepatic output of glucose (inhibit glycogenolysis).
30. Metformin causes less lactic acidosis, does not cause hypoglycemia, and is DOC for obese diabetic patients (MC-s/e-dyspepsia).
31. *Acarbose* is alpha-glucosidase inhibitor, can even be used in IDDM; ***hypoglyecemia*** is a mild problem. Its main use is in impaired glucose tolerance.
32. *Thiozolidinediones* (trogliatazone, piogliatazones) are insulin sensitizers.
33. *Maglitinide* derivatives act in same manner as insulin (secretagogues).

ANTICANCER AND IMMUNOSUPPRESSIVE DRUGS AND TOXICOLOGY

1. Alkylating agents form covalent bonds, are radio-mimetic agents. Cause both apoptosis and necoris and causes is their most common side effect.
2. *Doxorubicin* is broadest spectrum anticancer drug, causes cardio toxicity (Dexrazone is DOC).
3. Cyclophosphamide causes hemorrhagic cystitis (MESNA is DOC and is given IV).
4. *Bleomycin* (MC-s/e pulmonary fibrosis) causes minimal bone marrow suppression (Busulfan-DOC for CML causes MAXIMUM suppression).
5. *Vinca-alkaloids* (vincristine and vinblastine) cause peripheral neuropathy (vincristine >>vinblastine). These are used in leukemia and lymphomas. Importantly, *vincristine* is free from bone marrow suppression effect.
6. Taxanes (paclitaxel, docetaxel) promote microtubule polymerization and are used in breast and ovarian cancers. Side effects are neuropathy and hypersensitivity. Bone marrow depression also occur.
7. Platinum compounds, e.g., cisplatin act in same manner as alkylating agents. Cisplatin is given as continuous IV infusion and is DOC for reproductive cancers (e.g., cervical, ovarian etc.). Side effects include nephrotoxicity, neuropathy, ototoxicity and bone marrow depression.

8. *Cyclosporine* is MC immunosuppressive drug, acts by binding to CYCLOPHILLINS and reduce expression of IL-2.
9. *Tacrolimus* binds to FKBP-12 and is free from hirsutism and gums enlargement.
10. *Azathioprine*, given with allopurinol should be used in reduced doses to avoid bone marrow toxicity.
11. *L-asparginase* causes pancreatitis and hypersensitivity reactions.
12. Amifostine is DOC for reducing anti-cancer drug associated toxicity.
13. *Dimercaprol* (BAL) has two SH groups, which interact with *sulfhydryl* containing enzymes in the body – CI in iron and cadmium poisoning.
14. EDTA is used in lead intoxication but not in Hg poisoning.
15. *Penicillamine* is used for copper, lead, mercury, zinc and is DOC for Wilson's disease; also DOC for cystinuria.
16. *Deferroxamine* (1 gm for 85 mg) is obtained from actinomycetes-iron chelator – MC side effect is hypotension on IV injection.
17. *Deferiprone*–New iron chelator for patients with multiple blood transfusion.

Unit 21

MCQs

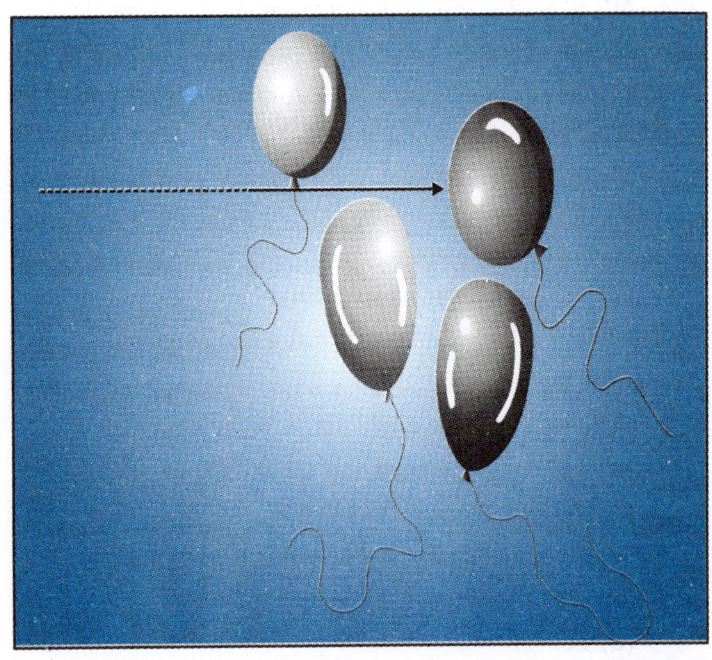

I hear, I forget
I see, I remember
I do, I understand.
— Chinese Proverb

1. **Dose of 6-mercaptopurine reduced with:**
   (a) Azathioprine
   (b) 6-thiogaunine
   (c) 6-mercaptopurine
   (d) Vitamin B_6
   (e) Allopurinol
2. **Which of the following is cardiotoxic?**
   (a) 5-FU
   (b) Bleomycin
   (c) Vincristine
   (d) Adriamycin (Doxorubicin)
3. **Which of the following is not a use of griseofulvin?**
   (a) Tinea capitis
   (b) Tinea versicolor
   (c) Tinea corporis
   (d) Tinea ungium
4. **Which of the following is wrongly matched?**
   (a) Iron-Desferroxamine
   (b) Lead-Penicillamine
   (c) Morphine-Atropine
   (d) Cyanide-Sodium thiosulphate
5. **Non-potassium sparing diuretic is:**
   (a) Triamterene
   (b) Amiloride
   (c) Spironolactone
   (d) Ethacrynic acid

6. **Steroid preparation which can be given by inhalation is:**
   (a) Beclomethasone
   (b) Hydrocortisone
   (c) Budesonide
   (d) Methylprednisolone
7. **All hepatic abnormalities are seen with oral contraceptive pill, except:**
   (a) Angiosarcoma
   (b) Cirrhosis
   (c) Budd Chiari syndrome
   (d) Hepatic adenoma
8. **Hypersensitive cholestatic jaundice is caused by:**
   (a) Cephalosporins
   (b) Erythromycin
   (c) Amoxicillin
   (d) Ampicillin
9. **All of the following cross placenta, except:**
   (a) Warfarin
   (b) Heparin
   (c) Morphine
   (d) Pethidine
10. **Main action of digoxin includes all, except:**
    (a) Increases heart rate
    (b) Increases cardiac output
    (c) Decreases peripheral resistance
    (d) Decreases size of heart

11. **All are adverse effects of digitalis, except:**
    (a) Ventricular tachycardia
    (b) Vasodilation
    (c) Nausea and vomiting
    (d) Pulsus bigeminus
12. **Which of the following is not an inducer of hepatic microsomal enzymes:**
    (a) Phenytoin
    (b) Meprobamate
    (c) Tolbutamide
    (d) Rifampicin
13. **Danazole has been used in the treatment of all, except:**
    (a) Uterine fibroid
    (b) Hirsutism
    (c) Endometriosis
    (d) Dysfunctional uterine bleeding
14. **Most important indication of calcitonin is:**
    (a) Hyperparathyroidism
    (b) Vitamin D intoxication
    (c) Paget's disease
    (d) Otosclerosis
15. **Which is not a ganglion blocker:**
    (a) Hexamethonium
    (b) Halothane
    (c) Trimethaphan
    (d) Mecylamine

16. In 32nd week of pregnancy with severe hypertension what drug not to be used:

(a) Furosemide

(b) Nifedipine

(c) Labetalol

(d) Methyldopa

17. Which is wrong about calcium channel blockers:

(a) Verapamil is useful in sick sinus syndrome

(b) Nifedipine is useful in exercise-induced asthma

(c) Nifedipine is good for CHF

(d) Verapamil has good anti-arrhythmic action

18. All of the following causes peripheral neuritis, except:

(a) Vincristine therapy

(b) INH therapy

(c) Folic acid deficiency

(d) Chronic alcoholism

19. Which of the following is drug of choice for intestinal amoebiasis:

(a) Chloroquine

(b) Emetine

(c) Metronidazole

(d) Diloxanide furate

20. Which is not a feature of opiate withdrawal:

(a) Insomnia

(b) Piloerection

(c) Constipation

(d) Rhinorrhea

21. **Dose of digoxin is reduced in all, except:**
    (a) Hypokalemia
    (b) Hepatic disease
    (c) Old persons
    (d) Hypoxia
22. **Hydroxyethyl starch is a:**
    (a) Vasodilator
    (b) Plasma expander
    (c) Inotropic agent
    (d) Type of dextran
23. **In case of diabetes mellitus, lactic acidosis is due to:**
    (a) Androstenedione
    (b) Sulphonylureas
    (c) Phenformin
    (d) Metformin
24. **All of the following cross plasma membrane, except:**
    (a) Androstenedione
    (b) Alpha-methyl-dopa
    (c) Epinephrine
    (d) Thyroxine
25. **In proximal convoluted tubule, sodium reabsorption is prevented by:**
    (a) Triamterene
    (b) Acetazolamide
    (c) Ethacrynic acid
    (d) Mannitol

26. Mebendazole is used in all, except:
(a) Strongyloides starcoralis
(b) Hook worm
(c) Round worm
(d) Trichuris trichura

27. Emetic action of morphine is due to action on:
(a) Gastric mucosa
(b) Chemoreceptor trigger zone (CTZ)
(c) Vomiting center in medulla
(d) Unknown mechanism

28. Most potent cardiac stimulant among the following is:
(a) Isoprotelanol
(b) Adrenaline
(c) Noradrenaline
(d) Salbutamol

29. Cyclosporine acts on:
(a) B lymphocytes
(b) CD8+cells
(c) CD4+cells (d) CD16+cells

30. Omeprazole lacts by:
(a) Modifying CAMP
(b) Inhibiting proton pump
(c) Inhibiting phospholipase
(d) Stabilizing membrane
(e) None of the above

31. Corticosteroid acts by:

(a) Inhibiting thromboxane
(b) Preventing degranulation
(c) Cyclooxygenase inhibition
(d) Preventing membrane phospholipase action

32. Anticancer drug crossing blood brain barrier is:

(a) Cisplatin
(b) Nitrosourea
(c) Doxorubicin
(d) Vincristine

33. Dopamine ts beneficial in shock, because:

(a) Dilates renal and mesenteric vessels
(b) Inotropic action on heart
(c) Constricts blood vessels
(d) Chronotropic action on heart

34. Drug of choice for petit mal epilepsy:

(a) Carbamazepine
(b) Phenytoin
(c) Ethosuximide
(d) Phenobarbitone

35. Which is not a hepatic inducer:

(a) Phenytoin
(b) Alcohol
(c) Rifampicin
(d) Tolbutamide
(e) None of the above

36. Aspirin act by:
   (a) Lipooxygenase pathway inhibition
   (b) Cyclooxygenase pathway inhibition
   (c) cAMP activation by adenylate cyclase
   (d) Membrane phospholipase action

37. Botulinum toxin acts by:
   (a) Increasing synthesis of acetylcholine .
   (b) Decreasing secretion of acetylcholine
   (c) Inhibiting release of acetylcholine
   (d) Blockade of neuromuscular junction

38. Treatment of Herpes zoster is:
   (a) Cytosine arabinoside
   (b) Steroid
   (c) Acyclovir
   (d) Methotrexate

39. Dihydrofolate reductase inhibitors are all, except:
   (a) Cytosine arabinoside
   (b) Pyrimethamine
   (c) Trimethoprim
   (d) Pentamidine

40. Streptokinases is beneficial in thrombosis, because of:
   (a) Plasminogen activation
   (b) Cyclooxygenase inhibition
   (c) Prevents propagation of thrombus
   (d) Directly acts on thrombus
   (e) None of the above

41. Drug acting on RNA virus in vitro is:

(a) Vidarabine

(b) Methisazone

(c) Amantadine

(d) Acyclovir

42. M1 muscarinic antagonist acting on gastric mucosa is:

(a) Atropine

(b) Propantheline

(c) Pirenzpine

(d) Oxyphenonium

43. In hyperthyroidism, Lugol's Iodine acts mainly by blocking the:

(a) Uptake of iodide by the gland

(b) Release of thyroid hormone from the gland

(c) Oxidation of iodic ions

(d) Coupling of iodotyrosine residues

44. The following are opioid withdrawal-symptoms, except

(a) Insomnia

(b) Piloerection

(c) Rhinorrhea

(d) Constipation

45. Sodium cromoglycate:

(a) Is an orally administered bronchodilator

(b) Is effective in an acute attack of asthma

(c) Inhibits release of chemical mediators from mast cells
(d) Inhibits response of chemical mediators on bronchial smooth muscles

46. Antacids decrease the bioavailability of all the following drugs, except:
(a) Ofloxacin
(b) Ketoconazole
(c) Oxytetracycline
(d) Erythromycin

47. Following are true regarding lovastatin, except:
(a) It is a HMG CoA reductase inhibitor
(b) It is effective in reducing raised cholesterol
(c) It may produce myositis
(d) It cause lenticular opacities in humans

48. Primaquine is not a:
(a) Primary tissue schizonticide
(b) Secondary tissue schizonticide
(c) Sporonticide
(d) Gametocide

49. D-Penicillamine can be used In all of the following, except:
(a) Rheumatoid arthritis
(b) Wilson's disease
(c) Mercury poisoning
(d) Erythropoietic porphyria

50. The following drug can give rise to hypersensitive hepatitis:

(a) Doxycycline

(b) Pentazocine

(c) Nicotinic acid

(d) Pyrazinamide

51. DNA-dependent RNA polymerase of the bacteria is inhibited by:

(a) Warfarin

(b) Streptomycin

(c) Ciprofloxacin

(d) Rifampicin

52. Colchicine is used for treatment of following, except:

(a) Cirrhosis of liver

(b) Familial Mediterranean fever

(c) Adrenal adenoma

(d) Amyloidosis

53. Half-life of a drug is a good Indicator of the following, except:

(a) Time required to reach steady state

(b) Time for a drug to be removed from the body

(c) Appropriate dosing interval

(d) Margin of safety

54. Metabolism of theophylline is decreased by:

(a) Ampicillin

(b) Phenytoin

(c) Rifampicin
(d) Ciprofloxacin

55. Tamoxifen is given in patients with:
(a) Carcinoma ovary
(b) Carcinoma cervix
(c) Carcinoma uterus
(d) Estrogen receptor +ve CA breast

56. Flushing on consumption of alcohol is seen with:
(a) Sulfonamides
(b) Metronidazole
(c) Phenothiazines
(d) Penicillin

57. 17-OH progesterone estimation is useful in:
(a) Ambiguous genitalia in female
(b) Hypertension
(c) Obesity
(d) Precocious puberty in female

58. All are side effects of phenytoin, except:
(a) Hypotension
(b) Acne
(c) Glucose intolerance
(d) Nephrotic syndrome

59. In Lithium toxicity all organs are affected, except:
(a) Liver
(b) Heart

(c) Brain
(d) Kidney

60. Which of following drug causes altered taste sensation?
(a) Rifampicin
(b) Ciprofloxacin
(c) Captopril
(d) Quinoline derivatives

61. Find the drug whose toxicity decreases healing power:
(a) Thiotepa
(b) Cyclophosphamide
(c) 5-FU
(d) Nitrogen mustard

62. Which calcium channel blocker has maximum effect on heart?
(a) Nifedipine
(b) Verapamil
(c) Diltiazem
(d) Nimodipine

63. All are β agonists except:
(a) Methoxamine
(b) Salbutamol
(c) Metoproterenol
(d) Terbutaline

64. Digoxin induced arrhythmia is treated by:

(a) Quinidine

(b) Procalnamide

(c) Phenytoin

(d) Lidocaine

65. Antagonist of benzodiazepines is:

(a) Nalorphine

(b) Carbamazepine

(c) Naloxone

(d) Flumazenil

66. Haemorrhagic cyctitis is caused by:

(a) Cyclophosphamide

(b) Busulphan

(c) Prednisolone

(d) Melphalan

67. Verapamil is used in all, except:

(a) Angina pectoris

(b) Atrial fibrillation

(c) Ventricular tachycardia

(d) None of the above

68. All increase blood theophylline levels, except:

(a) Smoking

(b) Erythromycln

(c) Allopurinol

(d) Cimetidine

69. **Melphalan is used in:**
   (a) Multiple myeloma
   (b) Wilm's Tumor
   (c) Neuroblastoma
   (d) Retinoblastoma

70. **Tolerance occurs to all side effects of morphine, except:**
   (a) Sedation
   (b) Constipation
   (c) Pain relieving
   (d) Euphoric effect
   (e) None of the above.

71. **All are contraindications for use of streptokinase in management of MI, except:**
   (a) Active peptic ulcer
   (b) Coagulopathy
   (c) NIDDM
   (d) Hypotension

72. **α-blockers are not used in all, except:**
   (a) Hypertension
   (b) Thyrotoxicosis
   (c) Variant angina
   (d) All of the above

73. **Dose of Ketotifen is:**
   (a) 1-2 mg/d OD
   (b) 10 mg I/V

(c) 5 –10 mg BD ORAL
(d) None of the above

74. Skin pigmentation is caused by:
(a) Cyclophosphamide
(b) Dactinomycin
(c) Methotrexate
(d) Busulphan

75. Dapsone is used in the treatment of all, except:
(a) Rhinosporidiosis
(b) Actinomycetoma
(c) Dermatitis herpetiformis
(d) Leprosy

76. Which of the following does not cause bone marrow suppression?
(a) Daunorubicin
(b) Cisplatin
(c) Cyclophosphamide
(d) Vincristine

77. All are metabolized by acetylation, except:
(a) Hydralazine
(b) INH
(c) Procainamide
(d) Chlorpromazine

78. Long term use of nitrates lead to decreased effect because of:
(a) Development of resistance

(b) —SH group in the enzyme
(c) Decreased oral absorption
(d) Increased resistance

79. Photosensitivity is a side effect of:
(a) Ofloxacin
(b) Ciprofloxacin
(c) Norfloxacin
(d) Pefloxacin

80. Which drug has wide therapeutic index?
(a) Digoxin
(b) Lithium
(c) Phenytoin
(d) Penicillin

81. Most potent glucocorticoid is:
(a) Prednisolone
(b) Fludrocortisone
(c) Hydrocortisone
(d) Dexamethasone

82. Which of the following interacts with digitalis maximally?
(a) Furosemide
(b) Triamterene
(c) Amiloride
(d) Spironolactone
(e) None of the above

83. All are used in digoxin toxicity except:

(a) Lignocaine
(b) Hemodialysis
(c) Phenytoin
(d) Potassium

84. All are nephrotoxic except:

(a) Lithium
(b) Gentamicin
(c) Chlorpromazine
(d) Cephalosporins

85. All are used in management of hypercalcemia, except:

(a) Mithramycin
(b) Penicillamine
(c) Bisphosphonates
(d) Steroids

86. Which does not cause optic neuropathy?

(a) Penicillin
(b) INH
(c) Ethambutol
(d) Chloramphenicol

87. All are predominant arteriolar dilators, except:

(a) Diazoxide
(b) Minoxidil
(c) Hydralazine
(d) Sodium nitroprusside

88. Ganciclovir is used in treatment of:

(a) Adenovirus
(b) Cytomegalovirus
(c) EB virus
(d) Arenavirus

89. All are true regarding Ketorolac, except:

(a) Respiratory depression is a side effect
(b) More potent than Aspirin
(c) Effect is prolonged
(d) This is an analgesic

90. Absolutely contra Indicated anti hypertensive drug in pregnancy:

(a) Enalapril
(b) Diazoxide
(c) Atenolol
(d) Nifedipine

91. Which anti thyroid drug can be safely used in pregnancy?

(a) Propylthiouracil
(b) I^{131}
(c) Methimazole
(d) Carbimazole

92. Ciprofloxacin acts on:

(a) DNA histone protons
(b) DNA gyrase
(c) CAMP
(d) mRNA polymerase

93. Pulmonary fibrosis is a side effects of:

(a) Methotrexate
(b) Vincristine
(c) Bleomycin
(d) Cyclophosphamide

94. Therapeutic effects of theophylline is enhanced by all, except:

(a) Cimetidine
(b) Smoking
(c) Erythromycin
(d) Congestive heart failure

95. All are anxiolytic, except:

(a) Fluoxetine
(b) Buspirone
(c) Diazepam
(d) Nitrazepam

96. Drug used in treatment of carcinoma thyroid is:

(a) Doxorubicin
(b) 5 -Fluorouracil
(c) Methotrexate
(d) Vinblastine

97. Mechanism of action of clonidine in opioid withdrawal syndrome is:

(a) Beta blocking effect
(b) Inhibition of opioid receptor
(c) Action on alpha2

(d) Presynaptic nerve
(e) Postsynaptic action

98. Non-sedating antidepressant is:
(a) Fluoxetine
(b) Mianserin
(c) Amoxepine
(d) Imipramine

99. First-pass effect is seen with which route of administration:
(a) Oral
(b) Sublingual
(c) Intramuscular
(d) Intravenous

100. All are α-adrenergic agonists, except:
(a) Mepheneteramine
(b) Ritodrine
(c) Methoxamine
(d) Phenylephrine

101. All the following affect metabolism of theophylline, except:
(a) Erythromycin
(b) Smoking
(c) Cimetidine
(d) Steroids

102. Adrenal steroids are contraindicated in all except:
(a) Severe hypertension

(b) Osteoporosis
(c) Diabetes mellitus
(d) Cushing's syndrome

103. Which of the following drugs is known to cause vaginal adenocarcinoma in female offspring when given to a pregnant woman?
(a) Chlorpropamide
(b) Progesterone
(c) Diethylstilbestrol
(d) Chloramphenicol

104. Which drug has the least anti-cholinergic side effects?
(a) Imipramine
(b) Doxepin
(c) Fluoxetine
(d) Clomipramine

105. L-dopa is given along with carbidopa:
(a) To reduce peripheral decarboxylation of L-dopa
(b) To reduce side effects
(c) To increase compliance
(d) To increase half-life

106. All the following displace imipramine from protein binding sites, except:
(a) Aspirin
(h) Propranolol
(c) Glibenclamide
(d) Lithium

107. The dose of digoxin should be reduced when given along with:

(a) Quinidine
(b) Rifampicin
(c) Indomethacin
(d) Antacids

108. Rapidly progressive pulmonary fibrosis is seen in:

(a) Paracetamol poisoning
(b) Kerosene poisoning
(c) Amiodarone poisoning
(d) Chloroquine toxicity

109. A cardiotoxic drug is

(a) Adriamycin
(b) Cyclophosphamide
(c) 5-Fu
(d) All of the above

110. Digoxin toxicity can be precipitated by all, except

(a) Phenytoin
(b) Quinidine
(c) Calcium
(d) Verapamil

111. Tocainide has the following properties, except

(a) Used in ventricular tachycardia
(b) Prolongs APD
(c) Used as lidocaine analogue
(d) Used orally

112. Which of the following is the drug of choice for PSVT?
(a) Lignocaine
(b) Verapamil
(c) Flecainide
(d) Tocainide
(e) Adenosine

113. Furosemide causes all, except:
(a) Hyperuricemia
(b) Ototoxicity
(c) Hypercalcemia
(d) Hypokalemia

114. All the following are used in motion sickness, except:
(a) Cyclizine
(b) Hyoscine
(c) Domperidone
(d) Meclizine

115. The commonest side-effect of cisapride is:
(a) Abdominal cramps
(b) Diarrhea
(c) Headache
(d) Convulsions

116. Side effect of clofazamine are all, except:
(a) Skin pigmentation
(b) Gastrointestinal disturbance
(c) Ichthyoids
(d) Anemia

117. Megaloblastic anemia is a side effect of long-term therapy with

(a) Diazepam

(b) NH

(c) Phenobarbitone

(d) Lithium

118. Which analgesic is not used in acute myocardial infarction?

(a) Morphine

(b) Pentazocine

(c) Pethidine

(d) Buprenorphine

119. Dosage adjustment is not needed in renal failure in:

(a) INH

(b) Ethambutol

(c) Rifampicin

(d) Streptomycin

120. Gout is not caused by which of the following drug?

(a) Chlorthalidone

(b) Sulfinpyrazone

(c) Aspirin

(d) Pyrazinamide

121. Altered taste sensation is caused by :

(a) Pefloxacin

(b) Rifampicin

(c) Ciprofloxacin
(d) Captopril

122. Osteoporosis is a recognized feature of all, except:
(a) Early menopause
(b) Heparin
(c) Marfan syndrome
(d) Thyrotoxicosis

123. Which non-depolarizing agent is a ganglion blocker?
(a) Atracurium
(b) Pancuronium
(c) D-TC
(d) Gallamine

124. Drug absolutely contraindicated in pregnancy:
(a) Nifedipine
(b) Enalapril
(c) Diazoxide
(d) Atenolol

125. Drug which causes hypothyroidism is:
(a) Carbamezapine
(b) Lithium
(c) Sulphur
(d) Methotrexate
(e) None of the abovc

126. Bone marrow depression is seen with chronic administration of:
(a) Isoflurane

(c) Glycopyrrolate
(d) Chlorpromazine

137. Chloroquine acts on:
(a) Merozoites
(b) Blood schizont
(c) Tissue schiont
(d) Gametocytes

138. Extra pyramidal syndrome like side effects are seen in:
(a) Haloperidol
(b) Clozapine
(c) Tetracycline
(d) Ketoconazole
(e) None of the above

139. Aspirin is used in cerebrovascular accident because it:
(a) Inhibits TXA2 synthetase
(b) Alters RBC membrane
(c) Cycloxygenase inhibition
(d) Prostaglandin production inhibition
(e) None of the above

140. Opioid agonist-antagonist is:
(a) Pethidine
(b) Pentazocine
(c) Buprenorphine
(d) Methadone

141. Suxamethonium causes:
- (a) Jaundice
- (b) Splenomegaly
- (c) Atrial fibrillation
- (d) Muscle fasciculation

142. Therapeutic index of a drug is an indicator of its:
- (a) Potency
- (b) Safety
- (c) Toxicity
- (d) Efficacy

143. Side-affect of captopril are all except:
- (a) Cough
- (b) Hyperkalemia
- (c) Renal dysfunction
- (d) Hemolytic anemia

144. Which of the following is not true about enalapril:
- (a) It is a pro-drug
- (b) It is a di-peptide
- (c) It is more effective than captopril
- (d) Has less adverse effects
- (e) None of the above

145. Which drug causes osteoporosis on long-term use?
- (a) Estrogen
- (b) Progesterone
- (c) GnRH analogues
- (d) Warfarin
- (e) None of the above

146. Which of the following is not a catecholamines?

(a) Epinephrine
(b) Norepinephrine
(c) Dopamine
(d) Phenylephrine

147. Buprenorphine is a

(a) Partial agonist
(b) Pure antagonist
(c) Agonist-antagonist
(d) None of the above

148. Which of the following is false about pentazocine?

(a) Decreased vomiting and constipation as compared to morphine
(b) Risk of addiction is less than that with morphine
(c) Risk of addiction is more than that with morphine
(d) It is agonist-antagonist

149. Which of the following drugs act as mu receptors of the CNS?

(a) Morphine
(b) Buprenorphine
(c) Pethidine
(d) Pentazocine

150. Which of the following is not inotropic drug?

(a) Dopamine
(b) Isoprenaline

(c) Amrinone
(d) Amiodarone

151. Which of the following has the shortest plasma half-life?

(a) Propranolol
(b) Esmolol
(c) Timolol
(d) Atenolol

152. Which of the following does not cause thrombocytopenia?

(a) Chlorpropamide
(b) Phenobarbitone
(c) Quinine
(d) Thiazides

153. All the following drugs cause pulmonary fibrosis except:

(a) Busulfan
(b) Methotrexate
(c) Doxorubicin
(d) Bleomycin

154. Which of the following does not cause bradycardia?

(a) Propranolol
(b) Hydralazine
(c) Clonidine
(d) Reserpine

155. All the following antibiotics act on the cell wall, except:

(a) Ampicillin

(b) Bacitracin

(c) Cycloserine

(d) Griseofulvin

(e) None of the above

156. Advantages of 3rd generation cephalosporins over 1st and 2nd generation cephalosporins is that they are:

(a) B-lactamase sensitive

(b) Not orally administered

(c) Effective against Gram +ve bacteria

(d) Effective against Gram –ve bacteria

157. The following are true of fluoroquinolones, except:

(a) Low toxicity to host cells

(b) DNA-gyrase inhibitors

(c) Effective against pseudomonas

(d) Rapidly develop resistance

158. The anti-malarial drugs effective in pre-erythrocytic phase in liver are:

(a) Proguanil

(b) Chloroquine

(c) Pyrimethamine

(d) Quinine

159. Long term use of chloroquine does not lead to:

(a) Lichenoid eruptions

(b) Visual deterioration

(c) T wave changes in ECG

(d) Weight gain

160. Which of the following statement is false about acyclovir?

(a) It inhibits DNA synthesis and viral replication

(b) It is effective against influenza

(c) It has low toxicity for host cells

(d) Renal impairment necessitates does reduction

161. Following antimicrobial agents are used topically except:

(a) Clotrimazole

(b) Griseofulvin

(c) Nystatin

(d) Miconazole

(e) None of the above

162. Which of the following is not an amide?

(a) Procaine

(b) Lignocaine

(c) Bupivacaine

(d) Mepivacaine

163. Clindamycin acts by Inhibiting:

(a) Cell wall synthesis

(b) Protein synthesis

(c) Cell membrane synthesis
(d) Glucose utilization

164. Hyperlipidemia is caused by intake of:
(a) Calcium channel blockers
(b) Beta-blocker
(c) Methyldopa
(d) Reserpine

165. Gynaecomastia is side effect of all, except:
(a) Ranitidine
(b) Cimetidine
(c) Spironolactone
(d) Ketoconazole

166. All are used to treat hypercalcemia, except:
(a) D-penicillamine
(b) Corticosteroid
(c) Biphosphonate
(d) Mithramycin

167. Which drug is not given in Tenia solium infection?
(a) Niclosamide
(b) Praziquental
(c) Albendazole
(d) Flubendazole

168. All of the following causes hyperglycemia, except:
(a) Thiazide
(b) Diazoxide

(c) Theophylline
(d) Pentamidine

169. Which has maximum nicotinic effect?
(a) Bethanechol
(b) Carbachol
(c) Pilocarpine
(d) Methacholine
(e) None of the above

170. Theophyllines concentration is not interfered by:
(a) Rifampicin
(b) Clarithromycin
(c) Erythromycin
(d) Ciprofloxacin
(e) None of the above

171. Local anaesthetic which does not cause vasodilation:
(a) Lignocaine
(b) Cocaine
(c) Bupivacaine
(d) Tetracaine

172. Pulmonary fibrosis is a side effect of all, except:
(a) Busulphan
(b) Phenytoin
(c) Sulphonamide
(d) D-penicillamine

173. NIfedipine and beta-Blocker are given together:
(a) To decrease pedal edema due to nifedipine

(b) To overcome increased sympathetic activity of nifedipine
(c) Anti CHF action of propranolol
(d) Antiarrhythmic effect of nifedipine

174. Repolarization of ventricles is prolonged by which antiarrhythmic drug:
(a) Amiodarone
(b) Quinidine
(c) Lignocaine
(d) Procainamide

175. Zero order kinetics at a higher dose is seen with
(a) Phenytoin
(b) Heparin
(c) Probenecid
(d) Lithium
(e) None of the above

176. Examples of pro-drug are all except:
(a) Levodopa
(b) Omeprazole
(c) Enalapril
(d) Indomethacin

177. Lithium monitoring is done because of:
(a) Low therapeutic efficacy
(b) Very low therapeutic index
(c) Adverse effects
(d) Long half-life

178. All of the following anticholinesterases except:

(a) Physostigmine

(b) Ambenonium

(c) Pyridostigmine

(d) Echothiophate

179. Actions of atropine are all except:

(a) Bronchoconstriction

(b) Tachycardia

(c) Mydriasis

(d) CNS stimulation

(e) None of the above

180. Following are all true about Ipratropium bromide, except:

(a) Used by inhalation

(b) -IOP

(c) Dryness of mouth

(d) Scratching in trachea

181. Test for myasthenia gravis is

(a) Succinylcholine

(b) Edrophonium

(c) Atracurium

(d) d-Tubocurarine

182. It Theophylline is used with ciprofloxacin:

(a) Toxicity of Theophylline increases

(b) Efficacy decreases

(c) Activity of ciprofloxacin increases
(d) It decreases absorption of Theophylline

183. Amongst the following least glucocorticoid activity is seen with:

(a) Fludrocortisone
(b) Dexamethasone
(c) Triamcinolone
(d) Betamethasone

184. Flumazenil is:

(a) Benzodiazepine antagonist
(b) Benzodiazepine agonist
(c) Adrenergic blocking agent
(d) Cholinesterase inhibitor

185. N-acetyl cysteine is an antidote for poisoning due to:

(a) Paracetamol
(b) Dhatura
(c) Aspirin
(d) Propranolol

186. Buprenorphine is:

(a) Opioid agonist-antagonist
(b) Partial agonist
(c) Pure antagonist
(d) Partial antagonist

187. The most common side effect of chronic use of phenothiazine is:

(a) Akathisia

(b) Tardive akinesia
(c) Tardive dyskinesia
(d) Muscular dystonia

188. Drugs not used in myocardial infarction are:
(a) Inhibitors of platelet aggregation
(b) Thrombolytics
(c) Anticoagulants
(d) Inhibitors of plasminogen activator

189. All the following drugs decrease the preload except:
(a) Glyceryl tri-nitrate (nitroglycerine)
(b) ACE inhibitors
(c) Hydralazine
(d) Sodium nitroprusside

190. Food does not interfere in absorption of which of the following:
(a) Cimetidine
(b) Ranitidine
(c) Famotidine
(d) None of the above

191. All are examples of gastro kinetic drugs except:
(a) Cisapride
(b) Domperidone
(c) Erythromycin
(d) None

192. Acetylation is seen in all except:
(a) INH

(b) Hydralzine
(c) Procainamide
(d) Phenytoin

193. Which of the following is not a hepatotoxic drug?
(a) Ethambutol
(b) Rifampicin
(c) INH
(d) Cycloserine

194. All the following drugs are used in Pseudomonas infection, except:
(a) Pefloxacin
(b) Imipenem
(c) Aztreonem
(d) Vancomycin

195. ADH acts on:
(a) Proximal convoluted tubule
(b) Distal convoluted tubule
(c) Loop of Henle
(d) Collecting duct

196. All of following are examples of cardiotoxic drugs, except:
(a) Cyclophosphamide
(b) 5-FU
(c) Adriamycin
(d) Cisplatin

198. All of the following are calcium channel blockers, except:

(a) Nimodipine

(b) Verapamil

(c) Flunarizine

(d) Pirenzepine

199. Postural hypotension is common with:

(a) Prazosin

(b) Labetalol

(c) Sodium Nitroprusside

(d) Captopril

200. Drug which is contraindicated in pregnancy is:

(a) Tetracycline

(b) Erythromycin

(c) Ampicillin

(d) Chloroquine

201. Fastest acting drug in leprosy is:

(a) Rifampicin

(b) Dapsone

(c) Clofazimine

(d) Ethionamide

(e) None of the above

202. Carbamazepine is not used in:

(a) Mania

(b) Partial seizure

(c) Trigeminal neuralgia
(d) Migraine

203. Antidepressant, which is selective 5HT inhibitor is:
(a) Fluoxetine
(b) Imipramine
(c) Desipramine
(d) Amitriptyline

204. Drug causing icthyosis and hyperpigmentation, when used in leprosy is:
(a) Rifampicin
(b) Dapsone
(c) Clofazimine
(d) Ethionamide

205. Long term use of lithium causes:
(a) Peripheral neuropathy
(b) Hypothyroidism
(c) Anaemia
(d) Jaundice

206. Which drug is not effective in pseudomonas infection?
(a) Cefaclor
(b) Ceftazidime
(c) Cefotaxime
(d) Carbenicillin

207. Drug of choice of hypertension in pregnancy is:
(a) Methyldopa

(b) Thiazide
(c) Nifedipine
(d) Labetalol

208. All are true regarding prazosin, except:
(a) First dose effect
(b) Impaired glucose tolerance
(c) Selective alpha-1 blocker
(d) It is antihypertensive drug

209. Halofantrine is used for:
(a) Falciparum malaria
(b) Visceral leishmaniasis
(c) Leprosy
(d) Amoebiasis

210. Brombocriptine is not used in:
(a) Induction of ovulation
(b) Galactorrhoea
(c) Post pill amenorrhoea
(d) Luteal phase defect
(e) None of the above

211. All of the following cause macrocytic anaemia, except:
(a) Primaquine
(b) Methotrexate
(c) Trimethoprim
(d) Azathioprine
(e) None of the above

212. True about sufentanyl is:
- (a) Analgesic
- (b) Antibiotic
- (c) Anticholinergic
- (d) Newer antihistaminic

213. Drug of choice for pneumocystis carinii:
- (a) Cotrimoxazole
- (b) Erythromycin
- (c) Penicillin
- (d) Metronidazole

214. Digitalis acts in atrial fibrillation by:
- (a) Increasing AV node refractoriness
- (b) Decreasing AV node refractoriness
- (c) Both
- (d) Blocking Na^+K^+ ATPase pump

215. Androgen receptor blocking drug is:
- (a) Tamoxifen
- (b) Cyproterone acetate
- (c) Mifepristone
- (d) Nadrolone
- (d) Tibolone

216. Aspirin is used in AMI because it:
- (a) Decreases thromboxane synthesis
- (b) Has analgesic effect
- (c) Reduces prostaglandin synthesis
- (d) Reduces cardiac work

217. Which of the following is not a prodrug:
- (a) Lisinopril
- (b) Enalapril
- (c) Levodopa
- (d) Sullndac

218. Dose of which drug is not altered in CRF:
- (a) Rifampicin
- (b) Gentamicin
- (c) Tetracycline
- (d) Cephalosporins

219. Treatment of choice of acute migraine is:
- (a) Ergotamine
- (b) Sumatriptan
- (c) Propranolol
- (d) Paracetamol

220. Which of the following is not an example of cytochrome P 450 dehydrogenase inducer:
- (a) Phenobarbitone
- (b) Rifampicin
- (c) Phenytoin
- (d) Ketoconazole

221. All are features of ethambutol toxicity, except:
- (a) Retrobulbar neuritis
- (b) Colour vision defects
- (c) Hyperuricemia
- (d) Hypercalcemia

222. All are long acting bronchodilaters, except:
- (a) Salbutamol
- (b) Salmaterol
- (c) Terbutaline
- (d) Adrenaline

223. Gynaecomastia is a side effect of all, except:
- (a) Digitalis
- (b) Ketoconazole
- (c) Rifampicin
- (d) Spironolactone

224. Hyperuricemia is a side effect of:
- (a) INH
- (b) Rifampicin
- (c) Streptomycin
- (d) Pyrazinamide

225. Pneumopathy is a side effect of all, except:
- (a) Alpha methyldopa
- (b) Busulphan
- (c) Melphalan
- (d) Nitrofurantoin

226. All are dihydrofolate reductase antagonists, except:
- (a) Methotrexate
- (b) Cytosine arabinoside
- (c) Pentamidine
- (d) Pyrimethamine
- (e) None of the above

227. Dose of drug require no or minor adjustment in renal failure, except:

(a) Doxycycline

(b) Vancomycin

(c) Chloramphenicol

(d) Clindamycin

228. Peripheral neuropathy is a side effect of:

(a) Bleomycin

(b) Busulphan

(c) Cisplatin

(d) Doxorubicin

229. Antiandrogen is:

(a) Mifepristone

(b) Clomiphene citrate

(c) Flutamide

(d) Tamoxifen

230. Even in large dosages used in malaria, quinine does not cause toxicity, because:

(a) It enters in fat cells

(b) Elevated plasma alpha acid glycoprotein

(c) Deposited in infected RBC's

(d) Excreted rapidly in urine

231. "Hand foot syndrome" is an adverse effect of:

(a) 5-Flurouracil

(b) Bleomycin

(c) Etoposide
(d) Actinomycin D

232. Drug excretion through kidney depends on all, except
(a) High blood flow in kidney
(b) Molecular weight of drug
(c) Lipid solubility of drug
(d) Plasma protein binding of drug

233. Drug causing least physical dependence is:
(a) Alprazolam
(b) Fluoxetine
(c) Dextroproxyphene
(d) Pentazocine

234. Pralidoxime acts by:
(a) Reactivating cholinesterase enzyme
(b) Promoting synthesis of cholinesterase
(c) Promoting synthesis of acetylcholine
(d) Direct action on cholinergic receptors

235. Clonidine is a:
(a) a_1 selective agonist
(b) a_2 selective agonist
(c) a_1 selective antagonist
(d) a_2 selective antagonist

236. Propanolol is indicated in all of the following conditions, except:
(a) Thyrotoxicosis
(b) Varientangina

(c) Migraine
(d) Hypertension

237. Anti-Adrenergic drug which crosses the blood-brain barrier minimally is:
(a) Propranolol
(b) Atenolol
(c) Oxprenolol
(d) Alprenolol

238. All of the following are feature of sympathetic stimulation of heart, except :
(a) Contractility
(b) Heart rate
(c) Refractory period
(d) Conduction velocity increased

239. Antiulcer drug is:
(a) Pirenzepine
(b) Methyl cellulose
(c) Ciprofloxacin
(d) Pyrimethamine

240. Shortest acting neuromuscular blocking agent is
(a) Pancuronium
(b) Atracurium
(c) Mivacurium
(d) Vecuronium

241. Intracranial pressure may be increased by all of the following drugs except:
(a) Hypervitaminosis A

(b) Corticosteroids
(c) Quinolones
(d) Aminoglycosides
(e) None of the above

242. Which of the following antiepileptic drugs acts by the release of the Inhibiting transmitter GABA

(a) Valproic acid
(b) Diazepam
(c) Etnambutol
(d) Phenytoin
(e) None of the above

243. Furosemide and thiazide have similar properties in the following:

(a) Duration of action
(b) Site of action
(c) Effect on urate excretion
(d) Well absorbed orally
(e) None of the above

244. All of the following statements about antianginal action of nitrates are true except:

(a) Myocardial 02 consumption
(b) Both pre and after load
(c) Total pre and after load
(d) Cause favourable redistribution of coronary flow.
(e) None of the above

245. Which of the following antihypertensive drugs is devoid of any central action?

(a) Clonidine
(b) Methyl dopa
(c) Propranolol
(d) Indapamide

246. Interstitial nephritis is most commonly seen with:
(a) Methicillin
(b) Ampicillin
(c) Amoxycillin
(d) Cloxacillin

247. Maximum amount of Photosensitivity is seen with:
(a) Ciprofloxacin
(b) Ofloxacin
(c) Pefloxacin
(d) Norfloxacin

248. Administration of one of the following drug is known to result in neuropsychiatric symptoms:
(a) Rifampicin
(b) Cycloserine
(c) Ethionamide
(d) Cephalosporine

249. Most common side effect of 5-fluoro-uracil is:
(a) G.I. toxicity
(b) Bone marrow depression
(c) Cardiotoxicity
(d) Neurotoxicity

250. True statement about omeprazole is:

(a) It may cause Leiomyosarcoma

(b) It is a nitrosourea

(c) May induce carcinoid tumours in rats

(d) It is more frequently used by the I.V. route than orally

251. Which antiarrhythmic in not class IC agent:

(a) Propafenone

(b) Tocainide

(c) Flecainide

(d) Encainide

252. Which NSAID undergoes enterohepatic circulation?

(a) Phenylbutazone

(b) Aspirin

(c) Ibuprofen

(d) Piroxicam

253. 200 mg of a drug given I.V. has a peak plasma value of 40 micrograms/ml. What is the volume of distribution?

(a) 0.5 litre

(b) 1 litre

(c) 5 litre

(d) None

254. Which of the following is not true about benzodiazepines?

(a) Acts on GABA receptor complex

(b) Midazolam is shortest acting
(c) Nitrazepam decreases REM sleep
(d) Flumazenil is a specific antagonist

255. All of the following drugs are metabolized by acetylation, except:
(a) INH
(b) Dapsone
(c) Procainamide
(d) Metoclopramide

256. GpIIb/IIIa antagonist all, except:
(a) Abciximab
(b) Clopidogrel
(c) Tirofiban
(d) Eptifibatide

257. Which is not a prodrug?
(a) Ticlopidine
(b) Aspirin
(c) Clopidogrel
(d) Dipyridamole

258. Morphine causes all, except:
(a) Peripheral vasodilatation
(b) Decrease intracranial tension
(c) Nausea and vomiting
(d) Decrease in gastrointestinal secretion

259. Beta agonist used in preterm labour causes all, except:
(a) Hyperkalemia

(b) Hyperglycemia
(c) Tachycardia
(d) Relaxation of uterine muscles

260. All of the following are hepatic enzyme inducers, except:
(a) Phenobarbitone
(b) Erythromycin
(c) Griseofulvin
(d) Rifampicin

261. Pharmacogenetics is important in metabolism of
(a) Rifampicin
(b) Isoniazid
(c) Digitalis
(d) Propranolol

262. True statement about clonidine all, except:
(a) Increases parasympathetic outflow
(b) Decreases sympathetic outflow by stimulating central alpha receptors
(c) Not used in HTN
(d) Prazosin is used to antagonize side effects of clonidine

263. False statement about selegiline is:
(a) It is a MAO-A inhibitor
(b) Does not cause cheese reaction
(c) May be used in on-off phenomenon
(d) It is used in parkinsonism

264. A patient on phenytoin for the treatment of seizures develops depression for which he is prescribed tricyclic. He now complains of lassitude and his Hb reads 8; next step in managing this patient should be:

(a) Chest X-ray

(b) MCV should be estimated

(c) GGT should be estimated

(d) None of the above.

265. Which of the following drugs would be removed by dialysis?

(a) Digoxin

(b) Salicylates

(c) Benzodiazepines

(d) Organophosphates

266. Which of the following have receptors which are transcription factors all, except:

(a) Insulin

(b) Estrogen

(c) Glucocorticoids

(d) Vitamin D

267. All of the following statements about ticlopidine are true, except:

(a) Directly interacts with platelet membrane, GpIIb/IIIa receptors

(b) Onset of action is delayed

(c) Duration of action is long
(d) It is used as an alternative to aspirin in patients with cerebrovascular disease.

268. Used for the treatment of migraine, the triptans act through:
(a) 5HT-1A
(b) 5HT-1B
(c) 5HT-1F
(d) 5HT-3

269. All but one acts via GABA, except:
(a) Thiopentone
(b) Midazolam
(c) Zolpidem
(d) Promethazine

270. Regarding phenytoin, false is:
(a) Induces microsomal enzymes
(b) At very low doses, zero order kinetics occurs
(c) Higher the dose, higher is the half life
(d) Highly protein bound

271. Good Laboratory Practices are not a part of:
(a) Preclinical studies
(b) Phase I studies
(c) Phase II studies
(d) Phase IV studies

272. Which of the following is not used as a sedative, but causes sedation as a side effect:
(a) Antipsychotics

(b) Antihistamines
(c) Antidepressant
(d) Lithium

273. A drug X with high affinity to albumin is given I.V. binds with albumin, but not enough to saturate it. Another drug Y. also having affinity to albumin is given I.V. in concentration 150 times enough to saturate albumin. Which of the following happens:

(a) Tissue concentration of X increases
(b) $t_{½}$ of X decreases
(c) Volume of distribution of X increases
(d) Tissue concentration of X decreases

274. Mechanism of action of nitric oxide is:

(a) Increase cAMP
(b) Increase cGMP
(c) Increase IP3/DAG
(d) Non-adrenergic/non-cholinergic

275. All of the following utilize no, except:

(a) Hydralazine
(b) Sildenafil
(c) Glyceryl nitrate
(d) Minoxidil

276. True about benzodiazepines as compared to other hypnotics:

(a) They alter sleep pattern more than other hypnotics
(b) More sedative than other hypnotics

(c) Overdose is better tolerated compared to other hypnotics
(d) All of the above

277. All are pharmacogenetics conditions, except:
(a) Adenosine deaminase deficiency
(b) Malignant hyper-pyrexia
(c) Coumarin insensitivity
(d) G-6-PD deficiency

278. Which of the following is true?
(a) As the concentration of a drug increases over the therapeutic range, the bound form of the drug increases
(b) The bound form is not available for metabolism but is available for excretion
(c) Acidic drug binds to albumin; and basic drug binds to α_1 glycoprotein
(d) Binding sites are non-specific and one drug can displace the other.

279. β-blocker with peripheral vasodilator action is:
(a) Carvedilol
(b) Propranolol
(c) Atenolol
(d) Acebutolol

280. 'Coronary steal phenomenon' is caused by:
(a) Dipyridamole
(b) Diltiazem

(c) Propranolol

(d) Verapamil

281. The nitrate which does not undergo first pass metabolism is:

(a) Isosorbide mononitrate

(b) Nitroglycerine

(c) Pentaerythritol tetranitrate

(d) Isosorbide dinitrate

282. Enalapril is contraindicated in all of the following, except:

(a) Diabetic nephropathy with albuminuria

(b) Single kidney

(c) Bilateral renal artery stenosis

(d) Hyperkalemia

283. A 6 yr. old child presents with malignant hypertension The drug of choice is:

(a) Na Nitroprusside

(b) Sublingual Nifedipine

(c) Furosemide

(d) Enalapril

284. Which of the following is not given in a patient with pheochromocytoma?

(a) Atenolol

(b) Prazosin

(c) Nitroprusside

(d) Metyrosine

285. Spironolactone is contraindicated with of the following:

(a) Enalapril

(b) Atenolol

(c) Verapamil

(d) None of the above

286. Neostigmine is a:

(a) Primary ammonium compound

(b) Secondary ammonium compound

(c) Tertiary ammonium compound

(d) Quaternary ammonium compound

287. Drug of choice in acute central anticholinergic syndrome is

(a) Neostigmine

(b) Physostigmine

(c) Tacrine

(d) 4-amino pyridine

288. Selective α_1-A blocker is:

(a) Prazosin

(b) Terazosin

(c) Tamsulosin

(d) Indolamine

289. All of the following are selective β_1 blockers, except:

(a) Atenolol

(b) Metoprolol

(c) Labetalol
(d) Betaxolol

290. 'Vigabatrin' a new antiepileptic agent acts by:

(a) GABA-antagonism
(b) GABA-T inhibition
(c) NMDA antagonism
(d) Carbonic anhydrase inhibition

291. All of the following statements are true about nitrates, except:

(a) It releases NO
(b) It causes vasodilatation
(c) It decreases A.V. conduction
(d) It has high first pass metabolism

292. All of the following are true about competitive inhibitor, except:

(a) Resembles chemically with the agonist
(b) Bind the same receptors
(c) Reduces potency
(d) Maximum level is not reached by increasing the concentration of the drug

293. On higher doses zero order kinetics is seen:

(a) Phenytoin
(b) Propranolol
(c) Lithium
(d) Probenecid

294. Duloxetine is indicated in all, except

(a) Painful diabetic neuropathy
(b) Fibromyalgia
(c) Mild to moderate depression
(d) Anxiety with insomnia

295. All are classified as reversible anti-cholinesterases, except:

(a) Ambenonium
(b) Physostigmine
(c) Pyridostigmine
(d) Echothiophate

296. In treatment of cardiac failure, dobutamine acts by all of the following mechanisms, except:

(a) α receptors agonist
(b) β adrenergic receptors agonist
(c) Dopamine receptor agonist
(d) Increasing force of contraction

297. Which of the following antiarrhythmics drugs causes prolonged repolarization of ventricles and ERP?

(a) Amiodarone
(b) Propranolol
(c) Verapamil
(d) Quinidine

298. All of the following are side effects of amiodarone, except:

(a) Pulmonary fibrosis

(b) Corneal micro deposits
(c) Thyroid dysfunction
(d) Osteoporosis

299. Which of the following statements regarding adenosine is not true?
(a) Used in PSVT
(b) Administered as rapid I.V. infection
(c) Has short lived side effects
(d) Di-isopyramide increases its therapeutic effect

300. Most commonly postural hypotension is seen with:
(a) Prazosin
(b) Nifedipine
(c) Atenolol
(d) ACE inhibitors

301. Flumazenil is a:
(a) Benzodiazepine antagonist
(b) Benzodiazepine agonist
(c) Adrenergic blocking agent
(d) Opiate antagonist

302. The most common side effect associated with chronic use of phenothiazines is:
(a) Akathisia
(h) Parkinsonism
(c) Tardive dyskinesia
(d) Muscular dystonia

303. All of the following may be seen with neuroleptic malignant syndrome, except:

(a) Hypothermia

(b) Altered consciousness

(c) Muscle rigidity

(d) Involuntary movements

304. Tetrahydrocannabinol is the active component of:

(a) Marijuana

(b) LSD

(c) Hashish

(d) Heroin

305. Pralidoxime acts by:

(a) Reactivating cholinesterase enzyme

(b) Promoting synthesis of cholinesterase

(c) Promoting synthesis of acetylcholine

(d) Direct action on cholinergic receptors

306. Clonidine is a:

(a) α_1 selective agonist

(b) α_2 selective agonist

(c) α_1 selective antagonist

(d) α_2 selective antagonist

307. Propranolol is indicated in all of the following conditions, except:

(a) Thyrotoxicosis

(b) Variant angina

(c) Migraine
(d) Hypertension

308. Anti-adrenergic drug which crosses the blood-brain barrier minimally is:
(a) Propranolol
(b) Atenolol
(c) Oxprenolol
(d) Alprenolol

309. All of the following drugs may be used for motion sickness, except:
(a) Hyoscine
(b) Dicyclomine
(c) Domperidone
(d) Scopolamine

310. Shortest acting neuromuscular blocking agent is
(a) Pancuronium
(b) Atracurium
(c) Mivacurium
(d) Vecuronium

311. Which of the following antiepileptic drugs acts by the release of the inhibiting transmitter GABA?
(a) Valproic acid
(b) Diazepam
(c) Ethambutol
(d) Phenytoin

312. Drug of choice in PSVT is:

(a) Verapamil
(b) Propranolol
(c) D.C. shock
(d) Digoxin

313. Predominant arteriolar dilators include all of the following, except:

(a) Sodium nitroprusside
(b) Diazoxide
(c) Hydralazine
(d) Minoxidil

314. Which of the following antihypertensive drugs is devoid of any central action?

(a) Clonidine
(b) α methyl dopa
(c) Propranolol
(d) Indapamide

315. First drug to be used in anaphylactic shock is:

(a) Subcutaneous adrenaline
(b) I.V. corticosteroid
(c) Theophylline
(d) Antihistamine

316. Absorption of a drug depends on all, except:

(a) Half life
(b) Concentration of drug

(c) Route of absorption
(d) Vascularity of absorbing surfaces

317. The metabolism of a drug proceeding at a fixed rate regardless of any further increase in substrate concentration is:
(a) Zero order kinetics
(b) First order kinetics
(c) Second order kinetics
(d) Third order kinetics

318. All of the following drugs reduce after load, except:
(a) Nitroglycerine
(b) Dopamine
(c) Hydralazine
(d) Sodium nitroprusside

319. Loading dose of a drug is given:
(a) When half-life of a drug is long
(b) When therapeutic index is low
(c) When drug follows first order kinetics
(d) When serum concentration is to be achieved rapidly

320. Which of the following feature differentiates pethidine from morphine:
(a) Local anaesthetic action
(b) More analgesic action
(c) More respiratory depression
(d) Suppresses cough effectively

321. Exogenous adrenaline is metabolized by:

(a) AchE

(b) COMT

(c) Decarboxylase

(d) Acetyl transferase

322. Fluoxetine causes all, except:

(a) Diarrhea

(b) Insomnia

(c) Sedation

(d) Anxiety

323. Tardive dyskinesia is seen with:

(a) Anti-parkinsonism drugs

(b) Anti-psychotics

(c) Anti-epileptics

(d) Chronic alcoholism

324. Epinephrine causes hyperglycemia by:

(a) Increased glucagon

(b) Decreased insulin secretion

(c) Increased glucocorticoids

(d) Increased thyroxine

325. Steady state plasma level is achieved after:

(a) 2-3 plasma half lives

(b) 3-4 plasma half lives

(c) 4-5 plasma half lives

(d) 10 plasma half lives

326. Katanserin:

(a) $5HT_{1B}$ antagonist
(b) $5HT_2$ antagonist
(c) $5HT_{1A}$ agonist
(d) $5HT_{1D}$ antagonist

327. Bioavailability of drug depends on:

(a) Disintegration of drug
(b) Dissolution of drug
(c) Particle size
(d) All of the above

328. All are true about digoxin, except:

(a) Causes bradycardia due to increased vagal tone
(b) Acts by inhibiting Na^+K^+ ATPase in myocardial fibres
(c) It is 95 % plasma protein bound
(d) Primarily excreted unchanged by glomerular filtration

329. Atropine is useful in organophosphorus poisoning because it:

(a) Reactivates acetylcholine esterase
(b) Competes with acetylcholine release
(c) Binds with both central and peripheral acetylcholine receptors
(d) Is competitive antagonist of acetylcholine

330. Prostaglandin inhibiting action of aspirin is useful in treatment of all of the following conditions, except:

(a) Analgesia and antipyretic
(b) Closure of ductus arteriosus

(c) Uricosuria
(d) Anti-inflammatory and anti-platelet aggregation

331. Which of the following statement about drug action is not true?
(a) Competitive antagonist has no intrinsic activity but affinity
(b) Competitive antagonist has intrinsic activity and affinity
(c) Partial agonist has submaximal intrinsic activity and affinity
(d) Inverse agonists have affinity but minus intrinsic activity

332. Inter dose interval depends on:
(a) Half life of drug
(b) Dose of drug
(c) Age of patient
(d) Bioavailability of drug

333. Digibind is used to:
(a) Potentiate the action of digoxin
(b) Decrease the metabolism of digoxin
(c) Treat digoxin toxicity
(d) Rapidly digitalize the patient

334. Which of the following benzodiazepine is used as anxiolytic?
(a) Temazepam
(b) Diazepam

(c) Midazolam
(d) Clonazepam

335. Norepinephrine action at the synaptic cleft is terminated by:
(a) Metabolism by COMT
(b) Metabolism by MAO
(c) Reuptake
(d) Metabolism by acetyl cholinesterase

336. Which of the following is not an indication for oxytocin?
(a) Spontaneous premature labour
(b) Postpartum hemorrhage
(c) Uterine inertia
(d) Breast engorgement due to inefficient milk ejection reflex

337. Calcium channel blockers are useful in all, except:
(a) Angina
(b) Supraventricular arrhythmia
(c) Sick sinus syndrome
(d) Hypertension

338. The drug causing curare like effect is all, except:
(a) Chloramphenicol
(b) Polymyxin
(c) Tetracycline
(d) Streptomycin

339. Clofibrate, a lipid lowering agent inhibits both cholesterol and triglyceride synthesis by:

(a) Inhibiting HMG CoA reductase

(b) Bile acid binding, preventing its reabsorption

(c) Inhibiting VLDL production

(d) Activating lipoprotein lipase, resulting in VLDL degradation

340. Rimonabent is used in

(a) Obesity

(b) Hypertension

(c) Renal failure

(d) Diabetes

341. True about teratogenicity of a drug is all, except:

(a) It is genetically predetermined

(b) Environment influences it

(c) Related to then dose of the teratogenic drug

(d) Affects specifically at a particular phase of development of fetus

342. Both barbiturates and salicylates are maximally absorbed in stomach because:

(a) They are weakly basic and so highly ionized in stomach

(b) They are highly basic and so less ionized in stomach

(c) They are weakly acidic and do not ionized in stomach

(d) They are highly acidic and are highly ionized in stomach

343. Which of the following has least extrapyramidal side effect?

(a) Haloperidol
(b) Fluphenazine
(c) Clozapine
(d) Flupenthixol

344. Buspirone as compared to benzodiazepines:

(a) Is more potent anticonvulsant
(b) Does not interfere with GAB anergic transmission
(c) COPD
(d) Aphakia

345. Therapeutic index is indicator of:

(a) Safety
(b) Efficacy
(c) Potency
(d) Toxicity

346. Which one of the following is true about Phase II clinical trial?

(a) Large number of patients are included
(b) Efficacy
(c) Toxicity
(d) Safety

347. Xenobiotics involves all of the following enzymes, except:

(a) Hydroxylation
(b) Cytochrome oxidase

(c) Cytochrome P_{450}
(d) Methylation

348. Regarding efficacy and potency of a drug, all are true, except:
(a) In a clinical setup, efficacy is more important than potency
(b) In the log dose response curve, the height of the curve corresponds with efficacy
(c) ED_{50} of the drug corresponds to efficacy
(d) Drugs that produce a similar pharma-cological effect can have different levels of efficacy

349. All are reasons for reducing drug dosage in elderly, except:
(a) They are lean and their body mass is less
(b) Have decreasing renal function with age
(c) Have increased baroceptor sensitivity
(d) Body water is decreased

350. Untrue about fenoldopam
(a) Dopamine agonist
(b) Dopamine antagonist
(c) Sympathomimetic drug
(d) Used in hypertensive emergencies

351. The common side effect with fluoxetine therapy is:
(a) Seizure
(b) Anxiety
(c) Hypotension
(d) Loose stools

352. All of the following drugs are protease inhibitors except:

(a) Nelfinavir

(b) Saquinavir

(c) Abacavir

(d) Ritonavir

353. All of the following antibacterial agents act by inhibiting cell wall synthesis, except:

(a) Carbapenems

(b) Monobactams

(c) Cephamycins

(d) Nitrofurantoin

354. A diabetic patient developed cellutitis due to Staphylococcus aureus, which was found to be Methicillin resistant on the antibiotic sensitivity testing. All the following antibiotics will be appropriate except:

(a) Vancomycin

(b) Imipenem

(c) Teichoplanin

(d) Linezolid

355. Emergency contraception prevents pregnancy by all of the following mechanisms, except:

(a) Delaying/inhibiting ovulation

(b) Inhibiting fertilization

(c) Preventing implantation of the fertilized egg

(d) Interrupting an early pregnancy

356. Misoprostol is a:

(a) Prostaglandin E1 analogue

(b) Prostaglandin E2 analogue

(c) Prostaglandin antagonist

(d) Antiprogestin

357. Bisphosphonates act by:

(a) Increasing the osteoid formation

(b) Increasing the mineralisation of osteoid

(c) Decreasing the osteoclast mediated resorption of bone

(d) Decreasing the parathyroid hormone secretion

358. Which one of the following antibacterials should not be used with d-tubocurarine?

(a) Norfloxacin

(b) Streptomycin

(c) Doxycycline

(d) Cefotaxime

359. The following statements regarding benzodiazepines are true except:

(a) Binds to both GABAA and GABAB receptors

(b) They have active metabolites

(c) Decreases nocturnal gastric secretion in human being

(d) Extensively metabolized by CYP enzymes

360. One of the following statements regarding mycophenolate mofetil is incorrect:

(a) It is a prodrug

(b) It is a selective uncompetitive and reversible inhibitor of inosine monophosphate dehydrogenase

(c) It also inhibits calcineurin

(d) All are true

361. All of the following mechanisms of action of oral contraceptive pills are true, except:

(a) Inhibition of ovulation

(b) Prevention of fertilization

(c) Interference with implantation of fertilized ovum

(d) Interference with placental functioning

362. Which one of the following drugs does not interfere with folic acid metabolism?

(a) Phenytoin

(b) Gabapentin

(c) Phenobarbitone

(d) Primidone

363. Which one of the following drugs is LEAST LIKELY to cause constipation?

(a) Propranolol

(b) Verapamil

(c) Nitroglycerin

(d) Pentazocine

364. Which of the following drugs is not used topically for treatment of open angle glaucoma:

(a) Latanoprost

(b) Brimonidine
(c) Acetazolamide
(d) Dorzolamide

365. Which one of the following agents has been associated with hemorrhagic stroke?

(a) Phenylpropanolamine
(b) Terfenadine
(c) Quinidine
(d) Fenfluramine

366. Which enzyme is inhibited by aminophylline?

(a) Monoamine Oxidase
(b) Alcohol dehydrogenase
(c) Phosphodiesterase
(d) Cytochrome P-450

367. Which of the following is the muscle relaxant of choice in renal failure?

(a) Rapacurium
(b) Pancuronium
(c) Atracurium
(d) Rocuronium

368. All of the following are part of the treatment of Lithium toxicity, except:

(a) Treating dehydration
(b) Ingestion of polystyrene sulfonate
(c) Hemodialysis
(d) Using an antagonist

369. All are side effects of clozapine except:

(a) Granulocytopenia

(b) Seizures

(c) Sedation

(d) Extrapyramidal side effects

370. Which of the following is the drug of choice for treatment of corneal ulcers caused by filamentous fungi?

(a) Itraconazole

(b) Natamycin

(c) Nystatin

(d) Fluconazole

371. Which of the following drugs is not a part of the 'Triple Therapy' immunosuppression for post renal transplant patients?

(a) Cyclosporine

(b) Azathioprine

(c) FK506

(d) Prednisolone

372. All of the following cause hypertension except

(a) NSAID

(b) Erythropoietin

(c) Cyclosporine

(d) L-dopa

373. All cause interstitial nephritis except

(a) Diuretics

(b) β-lactam antibiotics
(c) Allopurinol
(d) INH

374. All are antiemetic except
(a) Domperidone
(b) Cyclizine
(c) Phentazocine
(d) Ondansetron

375. Which of the following in Imatinib mode of action?
(a) Competitive inhibitor of bcr abl gene product
(b) P glycoprotein inhibitor
(c) P glycoprotein stimulator
(d) Competitively antagonizes the ATP binding site

376. Maternal carbimazole intake causes all except
(a) Choanal atresia
(b) Cleft lip and cleft palate
(c) Fetal goitre
(d) Scalp defects

377. Drug used to prevent renal toxicity in case of alcoholic hepatitis
(a) Silymarin
(b) S adenosyll methionine
(c) Thalidomide
(d) Pentoxyphylline

378. Aplasia of the bone marrow not seen with:
(a) Methicillin

(b) Chloramphenicol
(c) Methyl hydantoin
(d) Chlorpromazine

379. Impotence is caused by which of the following drugs
(a) Angiotensin antagonists
(b) CCB
(c) b blockers
(d) ACE inhibitors

380. Which antitumor drug is not an alkylating agent?
(a) Cyclophosphamide
(b) 5-FU
(c) Busulfan
(d) Melphalan

381. True about Octreotide:
(a) Is active orally
(b) Is not a somatostatin analogue
(c) Used in secretory diarrhea
(d) Is a growth hormone agonist

382. Filgrastrim is used for:
(a) Neutropenia
(b) anemia
(c) Polycythemia
(d) Ncutrophilia

383. Which of the following is not an anticonvulsant?
(a) Phenytoin
(b) Flunarizine

(c) T opiramate
(d) Phenobarbitone

384. Which antiepileptic does not act via sodium channel blockade?
(a) Vigabatrin
(b) Carbamazepine
(c) Lamotrigine
(d) Phenytoin

385. All are true for immunosuppressants except:
(a) Sirolimus acts by T cell modification
(b) Tacrolimus inhibits calcineurin pathway
(c) Mycofenolate acts by inhibiting GMP dehydrogenase
(d) Cyclosporin is integral in transplant rejection regimen.

386. Which anticancer drug causes hypercoagulable syndrome?
(a) 5-FU
(b) L-asparaginase
(c) Melphalan
(d) Carmustine

387. Which of the following chemotherapy agent can cause syndrome of Inappropriate ADH secretion (SIADH)?
(a) Vincristine
(b) Vinblastine

(c) Dacarbazine
(d) Cyclophosphamide

388. Which of the following is an anti – pseudomonal antibiotic?
(a) Ciprofloxacin
(b) Vancomycin
(c) Cefaclor
(d) Tetracycline

389. A child is on beta-agonist for treatment of asthma. He may have all of the following except:
(a) Tremor
(b) Hypoglycemia
(c) Hypokalemia
(d) Bronchodilatation

390. Which of the following anticancer drug acts by hypomethylation?
(a) Gemcitabine
(b) 5-Fu
(c) Decitabine
(d) Homoharringotonine

391. True about heparin is all except:
(a) Prolongs aPTT
(b) Hyperkalemia is not seen
(c) Alopecia is seen
(d) Thrombocytopenia is seen

392. Drug causing maximal peripheral neuropathy is:
- (a) Zidovudine
- (b) Lamivudine
- (c) Stavudine
- (d) Didanosine

393. Which drug is not used for erectile dysfunction?
- (a) Phenylephrine
- (b) Apomorphine
- (c) Yohimbine
- (d) Vardenafil

394. High dose methotrexate is given in:
- (a) Osteosarcoma
- (b) Rhabdomyosarcoma
- (c) Retinoblastoma
- (d) Ewing's sarcoma

395. Which of the following is longest acting insulin?
- (a) Lispro
- (b) Insulin aspartate
- (c) Glargine
- (d) NPH

396. Naltrexone is used in a case of opioid dependence:
- (a) To treat withdrawl symptoms
- (b) To prevent relapse
- (c) To treat overdose
- (d) Addiction potential

397. A patient with active tuberculosis is being treated with INH and ethambutol as part of the overall regimen. Which of the following is the main reason for including the ethambutol?

(a) To facilitate entry of the INH into the mycobacteria

(b) To facilitate penetration of the blood-brain barrier

(c) To retard the development of organism resistance

(d) To slow renal excretion of INH to help maintain effective blood levels

398. Many therapeutic insulins are often modifications of "regular" insulin. The modifications include substituting some amino acids in the protein using recombinant DNA technology, conjugating insulin with NPH or combining it with zinc. For all these insulin, which of the following is the one common result of such changes?

(a) Elimination of allergic responses

(b) Enabling administration by either subcutaneous or intravenous routes

(c) Modification of onsets, durations of action

(d) Prevention of cellular K+ uptake as glucose enters cells

399. All are fibrinolytic, except:

(a) Streptokinase

(b) Urokinase

(c) Alteplase

(d) Epsilon aminocaproic acid

400. Best indication for use of abciximab is:
(a) Stroke
(b) Acute coronary syndromes
(c) Following angioplasty
(d) Deep vein thrombosis

401. Acamprosate is:
(a) Detoxifying agent for alcoholism
(b) Used for decreasing alcohol craving
(c) NMDA agonist
(d) Used in opioid poisoning

402. Adalimumab is:
(a) TNF-alpha antagonist
(b) Ant-IgG antibody
(c) EGF antagonist
(d) VEGF antagonist

403. Aliskiren is:
(a) Renin antagonist
(b) Renin synthesis inhibitor
(c) Renin modulator
(d) Renin releaser

404. Anagrelide is:
(a) Antiplatelet drug
(b) Platelet maturation inhibitor
(c) Anticancer drug
(d) Antibiotic

405. Aprepitant is:

(a) Antibiotic
(b) Anticancer drug
(c) Immunosuppressive
(d) Antiemetic

406. Capecitabine is mainly used for:

(a) Breast and colorectal cancer
(b) Lung cancer
(c) Skin cancer
(d) Testicular cancer

407. Cetrorelix is:

(a) GnRH analog
(b) GnRH antagonist
(c) Both
(d) None

408. Cinacalcet is:

(a) Calcimimetics agent used in CRF (chronic renal failure)
(b) Newer calcium lowering agent
(c) Used in osteoporosis
(d) Antipyretic

409. Dalbavancin is:

(a) Short acting
(b) Long acting
(c) Ineffective against Gram-positive infections
(d) Non glycopeptide

410. Viral entry blocker is:

(a) Enfuvirtide

(b) Anagrelide

(c) Atomoxetine

(d) Daclizumab

411. Exenatide and pramlintide are:

(a) Antidiabetic agents

(b) Antipyretics

(c) NSAIDs

(d) Newer corticosteroids

412. Ezetimibe is:

(a) Bile acid binding drug

(b) Cholesterol absorption inhibitor

(c) Newer statin

(d) Fibrate

413. Febuxostat is:

(a) Newer xanthine oxidase inhibitor

(b) Uricosuric drug

(c) Inhibits mitotic spindle

(d) NSAID

414. Flavopiridol is:

(a) Newer D2 blocker

(b) NSAID

(c) Anti proliferative drug

(d) Antiemetic

415. Linezolid is not useful in:
(a) Gram-positive infections
(b) VRE
(c) VRSA
(d) Pseudomonas

416. MALARONE is used for:
(a) Prophylaxis of malaria among travelers
(b) Treatment of malaria
(c) Malaria in pregnancy
(d) Treatment of malaria among travelers

417. Muromonab is:
(a) OKT3
(c) Antidepressant
(b) Antiepileptic
(d) NSAID

418. Pemetrexed is used in:
(a) Malignant mesothelioma
(b) Small cell lung cancer
(c) Non-small cell lung cancer
(d) Superficial cancer of urinary bladder

419. Not prolonging QT interval:
(a) Quetiapine
(b) Sertindole
(c) Lumefentrine
(d) Artemisinins

420. Drug used for "secondarily infected dermatitis" (SID):

(a) Retapamulin
(b) Rimonabant
(c) Ramelteon
(d) Ropinirole

421. Not true about rituximab:

(a) Used in B-cell lymphomas
(b) Anti-CD20
(c) Infusion-related side effects occur
(d) Used in asthma

422. Not used in Alzheimer's disease:

(a) Memantine
(b) Galantamine
(c) Donepezil
(d) Cevimeline

423. Rotigotine is:

(a) Dopamine agonist
(b) Dopamine antagonist
(c) Both
(d) None

424. Ruboxistaurin is:

(a) Protein kinase inhibitor used in diabetic complications
(b) NSAID
(c) Antibiotic
(d) Anticancer

425. Drug used in constipation:

(a) Rifaximin
(b) Rifabutin
(c) Riluzole
(d) Tegaserod

ANSWERS

1. (e)	2. (d)	3. (b)	4. (c)	5. (d)
6. (a) (c)	7. (a)	8. (b)	9. (b)	10. (a)
11. (b)	12. (c)	13. (b)	14. (c)	15. (b)
16. (a)	17. (b)	18. (c)	19. (d)	20. (c)
21. (b)	22. (b)	23. (c)	24. (b)	25. (b)
26. (a)	27. (b)	28. (a)	29. (c)	30. (b)
31. (d)	32. (b)	33. (a)	34. (a)	35. (d)
36. (b)	37. (b)	38. (c)	39. (d)	40. (e)
41. (b)	42. (c)	43. (b)	44. (d)	45. (c)
46. (a)	47. (d)	48. (d)	49. (d)	50. (c)
51. (d)	52. (a) (c)	53. (d)	54. (b) (c)	55. (d)
56. (b)	57. (a)	58. (d)	59. (b)	60. (c)
61. (c)	62. (b)	63. (a)	64. (d)	65. (d)
66. (a)	67. (c)	68. (a)	69. (a)	70. (b)
71. (c)	72. (a)	73. (a)	74. (d)	75. (a)
76. (d)	77. (d)	78. (b)	79. (d)	80. (d)
81. (d)	82. (a)	83. (b)	84. (c)	85. (b)
86. (a)	87. (d)	88. (b)	89. (c)	90. (a)

91. (a)	92. (b)	93. (c)	94. (b)	95. (a)
96. (a)	97. (c)	98. (a)	99. (a)	100. (b)
101. (d)	102. (a)	103. (c)	104. (c)	105. (a)
106. (b)	107. (a)	108. (c)	109. (a)	110. (a)
111. (b)	112. (e)	113. (c)	114. (c)	115. (a)
116. (d)	117. (c)	118. (b) (c)	119. (c)	120. (b)
121. (d)	122. (b)	123. (c)	124. (b)	125. (b)
126. (b)	127. (c)	128. (c)	129. (a)	130. (a)
131. (b)	132. (b)	133. (a)	134. (c)	135. (b)
136. (b)	137. (b)	138. (a)	139. (a)	140. (b)
141. (d)	142. (b)	143. (d)	144. (c)	145. (c)
146. (c)	147. (a)	148. (c)	149. (a)	150. (d)
151. (b)	152. (c)	153. (c)	154. (b)	155. (d)
156. (d)	157. (d)	158. (a) (c)	159. (d)	160. (b)
161. (b)	162. (a)	163. (b)	164. (b)	165. (a)
166. (c)	167. (d)	168. (c)	169. (b)	170. (b)
171. (b)	172. (a)	173. (b)	174. (a)	175. (a)
176. (d)	177. (b)	178. (d)	179. (a)	180. (b)
181. (b)	182. (a)	183. (a)	184. (a)	185. (a)
186. (b)	187. (b)	188. (b)	189. (c)	190. (c)
191. (d)	192. (d)	193. (d)	194. (d)	195. (b)
196. (d)	197. (d)	198. (d)	199. (a)	200. (a)
201. (a)	202. (d)	203. (a)	204. (c)	205. (b)
206. (a)	207. (a)	208. (b)	209. (a)	210. (c)
211. (d)	212. (a)	213. (a)	214. (a)	215. (b)
216. (a)	217. (a)	218. (a)	219. (b)	220. (d)
221. (c)	222. (d)	223. (c)	224. (d)	225. (a)

226. (b) 227. (c) 228. (a) 229. (c) 230. (c)
231. (a) 232. (a) 233. (a) 234. (a) 235. (b)
236. (b) 237. (b) 238. (c) 239. (a) 240. (c)
241. (d) 242. (a) 243. (d) 244. (c) 245. (d)
246. (a) 247. (c) 248. (d) 249. (a) 250. (c)
251. (b) 252. (d) 253. (c) 254. (c) 255. (d)
256. (b) 257. (a) 258. (b) 259. (a) 260. (b)
261. (b) 262. (d) 263. (a) 264. (b) 265. (b)
266. (a) 267. (a) 268. (b) 269. (d) 270. (b)
271. (d) 272. (b) 273. (a) 274. (b) 275. (d)
276. (c) 277. (a) 278. (a) 279. (a) 280. (a)
281. (a) 282. (a) 283. (a) 284. (a) 285. (a)
286. (d) 287. (b) 288. (c) 289. (d) 290. (b)
291. (c) 292. (d) 293. (a) 294. (d) 295. (d)
296. (c) 297. (a) 298. (d) 299. (d) 300. (a)
301. (a) 302. (a) 303. (a) 304. (a) 305. (a)
306. (b) 307. (b) 308. (b) 309. (c) 310. (c)
311. (a) 312. (a) 313. (a) 314. (d) 315. (a)
316. (c) 317. (a) 318. (b) 319. (d) 320. (a)
321. (b) 322. (c) 323. (b) 324. (a) 325. (c)
326. (b) 327. (d) 328. (c) 329. (d) 330. (c)
331. (b) 332. (a) 333. (c) 334. (b) 335. (c)
336. (a) 337. (c) 338. (a) 339. (d) 340. (a)
341. (a) 342. (c) 343. (c) 344. (b) 345. (a)
346. (d) 347. (d) 348. (c) 349. (c) 350. (b)
351. (b) 352. (c) 353. (d) 354. (d) 355. (a)
356. (a) 357. (c) 358. (b) 359. (d) 360. (d)

361. (d)	362. (b)	363. (a)	364. (c)	365. (a)
366. (c)	367. (c)	368. (d)	369. (d)	370. (b)
371. (c)	372. (d)	373. (d)	374. (c)	375. (d)
376. (b)	377. (a)	378. (a)	379. (c)	380. (b)
381. (c)	382. (a)	383. (b)	384. (a)	385. (c)
386. (b)	387. (a)	388. (a)	389. (b)	390. (c)
391. (b)	392. (c)	393. (a)	394. (a)	395. (c)
396. (c)	397. (c)	398. (c)	399. (d)	400. (c)
401. (b)	402. (b)	403. (b)	404. (b)	405. (d)
406. (a)	407. (b)	408. (b)	409. (b)	410. (a)
411. (a)	412. (b)	413. (a)	414. (c)	415. (d)
416. (a)	417. (a)	418. (a)	419. (d)	420. (a)
421. (d)	422. (d)	423. (a)	424. (a)	425. (d)

MCQs: MORE THAN ONE CHOICE MAY BE CORRECT

1. **State true or false:**
   (a) The kidneys receive approximately 20% of the cardiac output
   (b) In healthy young adults approximately 130 ml/min of protein free filtrate is formed at the glomeruli
   (c) Non-protein bound drug of molecular weight < 66000 passes into the filtrate
   (d) Potentially saturable mechanism for active secretion of both acids and bases exist in the proximal tubule
   (e) Low lipid solubility favors tubular reab-sorption
2. **In pregnancy:**
   (a) Most drugs cross the placenta by active transport
   (b) Ionized drugs cross the placenta more easily than unionized drugs
   (c) Drugs that reduce placental blood flow can reduce birth weight
   (d) The fetal blood-brain barrier are not develop until the second half of pregnancy
   (e) The human placenta metabolizes endogenous steroids
3. **The following drugs are confirmed teratogenic, except:**
   (a) Alcohol
   (b) Warfarin

(c) Isotretinoin
(d) Paracetamol
(e) Ramipril

4. **State true or false: In pregnancy:**
   (a) Intestinal motility is reduced
   (b) Blood volume contracts
   (c) Renal plasma flow increases
   (d) Water soluble drugs have a larger volume of distribution
   (e) GFR falls down
5. **All the following drugs does not cross placenta, except:**
   (a) Heparin
   (b) Corticosteroids
   (c) Insulin
   (d) Sodium Valproate
   (e) Pethidine
6. **The drugs absolutely contraindicated in pregnancy:**
   (a) Phenytoin
   (b) Corticosteroids
   (c) Quinine
   (d) Warfarin
   (e) Beta carotenes
7. **The following drugs associated with erythema multiform:**
   (a) Phenytoin

(b) Cyclophosphamide
(c) Salbutamol
(d) Halothane
(e) Cotrimoxazole

8. **The following drugs can produce hemolysis in patients with G-6PD deficiency, except:**
(a) Dapsone
(b) Paracetamol
(c) Primaquine
(d) Cotrimoxazole
(e) Aspirin

9. **Phase 1 studies:**
(a) Done on animals for finding dose to be given in humans
(b) Always use oral route of administration
(c) Are usually performed in terminal patients
(d) Does not require the use of controls
(e) Are performed in normal healthy adult

10. **The autonomic nervous system is divided into Para-Sympathetic and Sympathetic Nervous System:**
(a) Anatomically
(b) By the effects they produce stimulation or inhibition
(c) By the kind of neurotransmitter they release
(d) By the receptors they contain at their endings

11. **Rationale of combining atropine and anti-cholinesterases in reversal of nondepolarizing neuromuscular – blockade:**
    (a) The antimuscarinic increases the rate of recovery
    (b) The antimuscarinic reduces muscarinic – receptor mediated side effects
    (c) Both
    (d) Neither
12. **Probably most important ion for transmission to the AV node:**
    (a) Sodium
    (b) Potassium
    (c) Chloride
    (d) Calcium
    (e) Magnesium
13. **Beta adrenergic receptor antagonist that also blocks alpha receptors:**
    (a) Timolol
    (b) Esmolol
    (c) Labetalol
    (d) Propranolol
    (e) Nadolol
14. **Cardiovascular effects of cholinomimetic:**
    (a) Negatives chronotropic
    (b) Vasoconstriction
    (c) Decreased Av nodal conduction velocity

(d) Negative inotropism
(e) All

15. **Which of the following actions of atropine is utilized for preanesthetic medication?**
(a) Mydriasis
(b) Antisecretory
(c) Vagolytic
(d) Respiratory Stimulation

16. **Vasomotor reversal of Dale is seen with:**
(a) Dopamine
(b) Adrenaline
(c) Nor-adrenaline
(d) All of the above

17. **Drug used in anaphylaxis is:**
(a) Norepinephrine
(b) Epinephrine
(c) Dopamine
(d) Antihistaminic

18. **Dopamine is preferred in treatment of shock because:**
(a) Renal vasodilatory effect
(b) Increased cardiac output
(c) Peripheral Vasoconstriction
(d) Prolonged action

19. **What is prodrug?**
(a) Drug which increases efficiency of another drug
(b) Metabolic end product
(c) Inactive drug which gets activated in the body

(d) Drug which completes with another for metabolism

20. Beta-blocker without local anaesthetic effect is:

(a) Metoprolol

(b) Pindolol

(c) Atenolol

(d) Timolol

(e) None of these

21. The difference between use of a selective alpha 1 blocker to using a non-selective alpha blocker is:

(a) Less reflux Tachycardia

(b) Decreased postural hypotension

(c) More vasodilatation

(d) Vasoconstriction

22. Tropisetron is useful in:

(a) Hypertension

(b) Glaucoma

(c) Cancer chemotherapy

(d) Peptic ulcer

23. Following are the unwanted effects of amphetamines:

(a) Insomnia

(b) Tremors

(c) Risk of dependence

(d) All of the above

24. Zilenton is:

(a) Selective lipoxygenase inhibitor

(b) Cyclo oxygenase inhibitor
(c) Angiotensin converting enzyme inhibitor
(d) Anticholinesterase

25. Epinephrine can be used in all of the following, except:

(a) Anaphylactic shock
(b) Chronic bronchial asthma
(c) Cardiac resuscitation
(d) To prevent local bleed

26. All of the following are actions of epinephrine on beta receptors, except:

(a) Tachycardia
(b) Ventricular arrhythmias
(c) A-V block
(d) Increased cardiac output

27. All of the following are true about succinyl choline, except:

(a) Causes persistent depolarizing block
(b) Metabolized by pseudocholinesterase
(c) Block can be reversed by neostigmine
(d) Has a short half life

28. Agents acting as antiemetic include all, except:

(a) Erythromycin
(b) Benzodiazepines
(c) promethazine
(d) Dronabinol

(e) Dexamethasone
(f) None

29. Examples of second messenger effect(s):
(a) Increases in cAMP intracellular concen-tration
(b) Changes in intracellular calcium concen-tration
(c) Phosphoinositide effects
(d) All the above

30. Major contraindications to the use of muscarinic agonists:
(a) Postoperative abdominal distension
(b) Asthma
(c) Treatment of diminished salvation, secondary to radiation
(d) Peptic ulcer
(e) Hyperthyroidism

31. Perioperative use of this selective beta adrenergic receptor antagonist in patients with significant underlying coronary heart disease may reduce the incidence of cardiovascular complication:
(a) Atenolol
(b) Propranolol
(c) Metoprolol
(d) Esmolol
(e) Timolol

32. Methoxamine-induced bradycardia could be blocked by administration of:

(a) Pilocarpine
(b) Labetalol
(c) Esmolol
(d) Atropine
(e) Edrophonium

33. Propranolol often decreases amide local anesthetic clearance by:
(a) Decreasing hepatic blood flow
(b) Inhibiting hepatic metabolism of local anesthetic
(c) Both
(d) Neither

34. This cateholamine simultaneously can increase myocardial contractility, glomerular filtration rates, sodium excretion, urinary output, and renal blood flow:
(a) Phenylephrine
(b) Isoproterenol
(c) Dobutamine
(d) Dopamine
(e) Epinephrine

35. Phenoxybenzamine (dibenzyline)–induced tachycardia could be blocked by prior administration of:
(a) Nifedipine
(b) Atropine
(c) Low-dose captopril

(d) Mecamylamine
(e) All of the above

36. Drugs from this class: effective in treating angina, arrhythmias and hypertension:
(a) Digitalis glycosides
(b) Alpha adrenergic blockers
(c) Angiotensin converting enzyme inhibitors
(d) Calcium channel blockers
(e) Beta adrenergic receptor agonists

37. Choose the ganglionic blocker:
(a) Propranolol
(b) Diazoxide
(c) Nitroglycerin
(d) Mecamylamine
(e) Phentolamine

38. Acts on vascular smooth muscle directly (arteriolar and venular): causes dilation probably mediated by nitric oxide; unstable in light; administered only by IV:
(a) Fosinopril
(b) Nitroprusside sodium
(c) Mecamylamine
(d) Phentolamine
(e) Nitroglycerin

39. Acts by depleting norepinephrine neuronal stores:
(a) Metoprolol
(b) Clonidine

(c) Captopril
(d) Guanethidine
(e) Phenoxybenzamine

40. Clonidine is indicated in all, except:

(a) Diarrhea in diabetics with autonomic neuropathy
(b) Preanesthetic medication
(c) Reducing hot flushes in
(d) Postmenopausal ladies
(e) Reducing craving for alcohol and narcotics

41. Potassium uptake by skeletal muscle is facilitated by the activating of:

(a) α_1 receptor
(b) β_1 receptor
(c) α_2 receptor
(d) β_2 receptor

42. The term receptor was introduced by:

(a) Paul Ehlrich
(b) Raymond Ahlquist
(c) Galen
(d) Hippocrates

43. Renin secretion is:

(a) Decreased by α_2 stimulation
(b) Increased by β_1 stimulation
(c) Increased by β_2 stimulation
(d) Increased by β_1 stimulation

44. Velnacrine, galantamine and donepezil are:

(a) Drugs recommended for Alzheimers disease
(b) Cholinesterase inhibitors
(c) Agents having mild cholinomimetic actions
(d) Antioxidants
(e) None of these

45. Benzodiazepines are all, except:

(a) Are the hypnotic of choice in most patients
(b) Can be given for long term usage
(c) Suppress REM sleep
(d) Act by binding to the GABA receptor –chloride channel complex and facilitate the opening of the channel in the presence of GABA
(e) Are anxiolytic

46. The following drugs can mimic some of the common clinical features of schizophrenia:

(a) Levodopa
(b) Salbutamol
(c) LSD
(d) Diamorphine
(e) MDMA, ectasy

47. Blockade of central D2-receptors:

(a) Parallels the clinical efficacy of antipsychotic drugs
(b) Induces extra-pyramidal effects

(c) Repeated administration of D2 antagonist causes an increase in D2 agonist sensitivity due to an increase in receptor numbers
(d) Causes a decrease in cardiac output
(e) Repeated administration may lead to tardive dyskinesia

48. Adverse effects of phenothiazines include, all except:
(a) Dry mouth
(b) Postural hypotension
(c) Cholestatic Jaundice
(d) Impaired temperature control
(e) Depression

49. Butyrophenones in comparison to pheno-thiazines are generally, except
(a) Less sedating
(b) Less hypotensive
(c) Less potent
(d) Less antimuscarinic
(e) Less extrapyramidal symptoms

50. Tricyclic antidepressant have all the following properties, except:
(a) Dilates Pupil
(b) Overdose cause hyperreflexia
(c) Widen QRS interval
(d) Anticonvulsant in higher doses
(e) May cause loss of antihypertensive effects of amethyl Dopa

51. **State True or False:**
   (a) Fluoxetine inhibit selective serotonin reuptake
   (b) Moclebomide is a new MAO-A inhibitor
   (c) Phenelzine is a reversible inhibitor of MAO-B
   (d) Amitryptiline is contraindicated in epilepsy
   (e) Mianserine is known for its bone marrow depression

52. **Lithium Toxicity can be precipitated by all, except:**
   (a) Thiazide diuretics
   (b) Hypernatremia
   (c) Hyperkalemia
   (d) ACE inhibitors
   (e) NSAIDs

53. **The following drugs/food/chemicals can cause hypertensive crises during MAO inhibitors, except:**
   (a) Cheese
   (b) Yogurt
   (c) Beer
   (d) Phentolamine
   (e) Amitrytyline

54. **Drugs enhancing dopaminergic activity**
   (a) MAO-B inhibitors
   (b) Bromocriptine
   (c) Apomorphine
   (d) Haloperidol
   (e) Intravenous Dobutamine

55. The following are the recognized adverse effects associated with Phenytoin therapy, except:

(a) Ataxia

(b) Dysarthria

(c) Acne

(d) Hyperkalemia

(e) Macrocytic anaemia

56. Vigabatrine is having all properties, except:

(a) A structural analog of GABA

(b) Increases the brain concentration of GABA

(c) First line treatment of Tonic-clonic epilepsy

(d) May cause hallucinations and paranoia

(e) Eliminated via kidney

57. Sumatriptan all are true, except:

(a) Bioavailability better after subcutaneous injection than oral administration

(b) Contraindicated in patients with IS

(c) May raise BP

(d) Can be combined with ergometrine in the treatment of Migraine

(e) Can be given with PCM in acute attack of Migraine

58. Atracurium:

(a) Is a non-depolarising muscle relaxant

(b) Has histamine blocking properties

(c) Metabolized in liver

(d) Dose need to be reduced in renal dysfunction

59. Steps useful in the treatment of malignant hyperthermia are all, except

(a) 100% oxygen administration

(b) Correction of metabolic acidosis and Hyper-kalemia

(c) i.v. dantrolene

(d) Rapid cooling

(e) Diazepam administration

60. Adverse effects associated with salicylates may include all, except:

(a) Claudication

(b) Bronchoconstriction

(c) Malena

(d) Hepatitis

(e) Reys's syndrome

61. Morphine can cause all, except

(a) Miosis

(b) Increased intrabiliary pressure

(c) Shift fluid from pulmonary to intravascular sites

(d) Binds to both CNS and spinal cord mu receptors

(e) Histamine release

62. Match the following for the specific antidotes:

(a) Morphine poisoning N-acetyl Glucosamine

(b) PCM poisoning citrate calcium carbide

(c) Barbiturate Poisoning Naloxone Hydrochloride

(d) Methanol intoxication Flumazenil

(e) Diazepam Poisoning Hemodialysis

63. Allopurinol may cause all, except:

(a) Inhibit xanthine oxidase
(b) May provoke acute attack of gout
(c) Precipitate renal failure
(d) Can increase the effects of azathioprine
(e) Useful in cases of kala azar

64. The following effects of colchicine are true, except:

(a) Inhibit the tubulin by preventing its polymerization
(b) Inhibit leukocyte migration
(c) Promote phagocytosis
(d) Inhibit the formation of leukotrine B4
(e) Useful in the treatment of acute gout

65. Leflunomide is used as:

(a) New immunosuppressive drugs
(b) New anticancer drugs
(c) Inhibit dihydroorotate dehydrogenase
(d) Latest antibiotic against staphylococcus
(e) Useful in treatment of Alzeimer disease

66. Which one of the following is long acting corticosteroids?

(a) Betamethasone
(b) Dexamethasone
(c) Methylprednisolone
(d) Triamcinolone
(e) Hydrocortisone

67. Non-adrenal indications of Glucocorticoids include:

(a) Allergic disorders
(b) Collagen vascular disorders
(c) Hypercalcemia
(d) Multiple myeloma
(e) Cerebral edema

68. Drugs useful as adrenocortical antagonist are all, except:

(a) Metyrapone
(b) Spironolactone
(c) Mifepristone
(d) Ketoconazole
(e) Aminoglutethimide

69. Side effects of hormonal contraceptives include all, except:

(a) Hyperpigmentation
(b) Migraine
(c) Osteoporosis
(d) Hypertension
(e) Cholestasis

70. Progestational drugs with no androgenic effects include all, except:

(a) Desogestral
(b) Norethynodrel
(c) Norethindrone
(d) Progesterone
(e) Norgestimate

71. SERMs (agents useful for treatment of postmenopausal osteoporosis) are all, except:

(a) Toremifine
(b) Raloxifine
(c) Clomiphine
(d) Tamoxifine
(e) Mifepristone

72. Mifepristone have all the following effects, except:

(a) Progesterone receptor blocker
(b) Suppress ovarian function
(c) Useful as a emergency postcoital con-traceptive
(d) Can be combined with Prostaglandin E1 for prevention of pregnancy
(e) Has Glucocorticoid agonistic activity

73. Ultrashort acting preparation of insulin include:

(a) Ultralente insulin
(b) Insulin glargine
(c) Insulin lispro
(d) Regular insulin
(e) Humulin

74. All of the following agents have insulin secre-tagogues action, except:

(a) Sulfonylureas
(b) Vagal stimulation
(c) Glucose
(d) Somatostatin
(e) Ripaglinide

75. Insulin sensitizers include all, except:

(a) Meglitinides
(b) Biguanides
(c) ACE inhibitors
(d) Thiazolidinediones
(e) Imidazoline agonist

76. Agents useful in the treatment of Osteoporosis include all, except:

(a) Raloxifene
(b) Alendronate
(c) Thiazides
(d) Corticosteroids
(e) Plicamycin

77. Match the Mechanism of action of the following agents:

(a) Penicillins	Inhibit protein synthesis (binds 50S submit)
(b) Tetracycline	Inhibit Cellwall synthesis (binds peptidoglycan)
(c) Linezolid	Inhibit Protein synthesis (binds 23S RNA)
(d) Sulfonamide	Reversible inhibitor of protein synthesis enzymes
(e) Aminoglycosides	Inhibitor in p-aminobenzoic acid

78. Drugs showing postantibiotic effects include all, except:

(a) Aminoglycosides

(b) Fluroquinolones

(c) Carbapenems

(d) Metronidazole

(e) Rifampicin

79. Drugs acting intracellularly include all, except:

(a) Isoniazid

(b) Rifampicin

(c) Ethambutol

(d) Pyrazinamide

(e) Streptomycin

80. Match the side effects of antitubercular drugs:

(a) INH	Retrobulbar neuritis
(b) Pyrazinamide	Peripheral neuritis
(c) Ethambutol	Crystalluria
(d) Rifampicin	Hepatotoxicity
(e) PAS	Orange colored urine

81. Drug of choice in the treatment of Pseudomembranous colitis is:

(a) Vancomycin (b) Metronidazole

(c) Amicacin (d) Clindamycin

(e) Tetracycline

82. Drug of choice in the treatment of CMV retinitis

(a) Acyclovir (b) Famiclovir

(c) Forscarnet (d) Ganciclovir

(e) Cidofovir

83. Compare the side effects of antiviral agents

(a) Penile ulcerations Acyclovir

(b) Myelosuppression Famciclovir

(c) Testicular toxicity Forscarnet

(d) Thrombiotic microangiopathies Ganciclovir

(e) Delirium Valacyclovir

84. Anti-HIV agents belong to non-nucleoside reverse transcriptase inhibitors include all, except:

(a) Zidovudine (b) Dilaverdine

(c) Efavirenz (d) Nevirapine

(e) None

85. Major side effects of anti-HIV agents include:

(a) Zidovudine Nephrolithiasis

(b) Didanosine Neutropenia

(c) Stavudine Pancreatitis

(d) Zalcitabin Oral ulcers

(e) Indinavir Peripheral Neuropathy

86. Drugs causing Peripheral Neuropathy include all, except:

(a) Stavudine (b) Zalcitabine

(c) Didanosine (d) Zidovudine

(e) INH

87. Drug useful in the radical cure of malarial infection include:

(a) Chloroquine (b) Mefloquine
(c) Primaquine (d) Proguanil
(e) Artemisinin derivatives

88. Drug of choice in the treatment of Chloroquine resistant Cerebral malaria:

(a) Mefloquine (b) Halofantrine
(c) Astesunate (d) Quinine
(e) Artemether

89. Drug of choice in the prophylaxis of cerebral malaria in a pregnant female:

(a) Quinine (b) Chloroquine
(c) Mefloquinine (d) Artemether
(e) Primaquine

90. All of the following antineoplastic agents are derived from natural source, except:

(a) Vinblastine
(b) Paclitaxel
(c) Etoposide
(d) Topotecan
(e) Methotrexate

91. Anti cancer agent acting in a cell cycle specific zone include all, except:

(a) Busulfan
(b) Bleomycin

(c) Vincristine
(d) Paclitaxal
(e) 6-mercaptopurine

92. All of the following agents inhibit topoisomerase enzyme, except:
(a) Ciprofloxacin
(b) Camtothecins
(c) Etoposide
(d) Paclitaxal
(e) Doxorubicin

93. Drug useful in the treatment of immune-related disorders include all, except:
(a) levamisol
(b) Tacrolimus
(c) Cyclosporin
(d) Methotrexate
(e) Thalidomide
(f) Leflunomide
(g) All of the above

94. Low molecular weight heparin differ from Heparin in all of the following, except:
(a) Binding site include factor X, but not AT-III
(b) Lesser efficacy, poor bioavailability of LMWH
(c) Useful in the treatment of acute coronary syndromes, acute venous thromboembolic diseases

(d) Low incidence of bleeding tendencies with LMWH

(e) Protamine is unable to completely reverse the effects of LMWH

95. Effects of warfarin include all, except:

(a) Block gamma arboxylation of glutamate residues –2,7,9,10

(b) Protein S

(c) Inhibit Protein C

(d) Reversal with Vitamin C intake

(e) Potentiated side effects in patients with deficiency of Protein C

96. All of the following agents are acting as antiplatlet agents, except:

(a) Aspirin

(b) Clopidogrel

(c) Abciximab

(d) Desmopressin acetate

(e) Eptifibatide

97. Drug acting as PPAR agonist include all, except:

(a) Pioglitazone

(b) Gemfibrozil

(c) Niacin

(d) Rosiglitazone

(e) Simvastatin

98. Match the following agents with their effects in treatment of asthma:

(a) Corticosteroids	5-lipoxygenase inhibitor
(b) Ipratropium bromide receptors	Inhibit muscarinic
(c) Zileuton	Increase cAMP levels
(d) Salmeterol	Leucotrine receptor antagonist
(e) Montelucast	Inhibit Proinflammatory cytokines

99. Drugs useful the treatment of NSAIDS induced peptic ulcer:

(a) Sucralfate
(b) Omeprazole
(c) Colloidal Bismuth
(d) Misoprostol
(e) Combination of Omeprazole with ranitidine

100. Ulcer healing agents are all, except:

(a) Proton Pump inhibitors
(b) H_2 receptor blockers
(c) Sucralfate
(d) Prostaglandin analogs
(e) Cabenoxolone

ANSWERS

1. (a)-T, (b)-T, (c)-F, (d)-T, (e)-F
2. (a)-F, (b)-F, (c)-T, (d)-T, (e)-T
3. (a)
4. (a)-T, (b)-F, (c)-T, (d)-F, (e)-F
5. (b), (c), (d), (e)

6. (d), (e) 7. (a), (e) 8. (b) 9. (e) 10. (a)
11. (b) 12. (a) 13. (c) 14. (b) 15. (b)
16. (?) 17. (b) 18. (a) 19. (c) 20. (d)
21. (b) 22. (c) 23. (d) 24. (a) 25. (d)
26. (c) 27. (c) 28. (a) 29. (d) 30. (b), (d)
31. (b) 32. (d) 33. (a) 34. (d) 35. (d)
36. (d) 37. (d) 38. (e) 39. (d) 40. (b)
41. (c) 42. (a) 43. (b) 44. (a) 45. (b)
46. (c) 47. (b) 48. (d) 49. (c), (e) 50. (b), (d)
51. (a)-T, (b)-T, (c)-T, (d)-T, (e)-F
52. (b) 53. (d)
54. (a), (b), (c) 55. (d)
56. (c) 57. (d) 58. (a) 59. (a) 60. (a)
61. all are true
62. (a)-(c), (b)-(a), (c)-(e), (d)-(b), (e)-(d)
63. (c) 64. (d)
65. (a), (c) 66. (a), (b)
67. (a), (b), (c), (d), (e)
68. (b) 69. (c) 70. (a), (c)
71. (c), (e)

72. (b), (e) 73. (c) 74. (d) 75. (c), (e)
76. (d), (e)
77. (a)-(b), (b)-(d), (c)-(c), (d)-(e), (e)-(a)
78. (d), (e) 79. (e)
80. (a)-(b), (b)-(c), (c)-(a), (d)-(e), (e)-(d)]
81. (b) 82. (d)
83. (a)-(c), (b)-(d), (c)-(b), (e)-(a), (d)-(e)
84. (a)
85. (a)-(b), (b)-(c), (c)-(e), (d)-(d), (e)-(a)
86. (c) 87. (c) 88. (d) 89. (a) 90. (a), (d), (e)
91. (a), (b), (e)
92. (d), (e) 93. (g) 94. (b) 95. (d)
96. (d) 97. (c), (e)
98. (a)-(e), (b)-(b), (c)-(a), (d)-(c), (e)-(d)
99. (b), (d)
100. (c), (d)